TheyHeal

Uniting in Love, Mental Wellness, and the Journey to Wholeness

By

R. Allure

For all of those lovely couples who are willing to make the leap into growth and healing together…

Foreword

And then it happened again… So, I had just released MENDIT – a mental wellness book for men and then I was asked for a similar book for ladies which was named SheHeals. And then what happens? Well, I have now had requests for a couples healing book to help navigate the path to mental wellbeing, love and growth for both parts of a couple whether heterosexual or homosexual. Now, please bear in mind I am not a therapist, in fact I work in technology and have brilliant AI at my fingertips. That means I can access vast realms of research instantaneously. In terms of writing books, well creative writing is one of my hobbies and I taught it for years. In addition, I am enthralled by the mind, personal development and achieving higher states of being. So, just to re-Iterate – I am not a therapist, instead I am curious about what I can discover about modern relationships, mental well-being and how we can navigate an entirely new relationship culture. Of course, I am going to have to add a disclaimer.

So here is it is:

Disclaimer

The information provided in this book, "TheyHeal - Uniting in Love, Mental Wellness, and the Journey to Wholeness," is intended for general informational and educational purposes only. The content of this book is not a substitute for professional advice or therapy, and it is not intended to diagnose, treat, or cure any mental health or relationship issues.

Readers are encouraged to seek guidance and support from qualified mental health professionals, therapists, or relationship counsellors if they are dealing with specific challenges or issues in their lives. The author and publisher of this book are not responsible for any actions taken by readers based on the information presented herein.

While every effort has been made to ensure the accuracy and reliability of the information in this book, the author and publisher make no representations or warranties of any kind, express or implied, about the completeness, accuracy, reliability, suitability, or availability with respect to the content. Any reliance you place on the information in this book is at your own risk. Now we have got that over with – let's lift our energy and enjoy igniting the relationship loving light:

TheyHeal

In the era of the heart, we find our way,
Two souls together, come what may.
We heal as one, hand in hand we soar,
In love's embrace, we'll forever explore.

Gone are the masks, the walls that hide,
In vulnerability, we stand side by side.
No judgment here, just love's sweet grace,
As we navigate life's intricate, sacred space.

Through trials and triumphs, we learn to be,
The best versions of you and me.
In this era of healing, we find our light,
Guiding each other through the darkest night.

We nurture our minds, our spirits mend,
A love like this has no end.
For in our togetherness, we truly see,
The beauty of love, pure and free.

So let us embrace this journey we're on,
In the era of the heart, where love is drawn.
Healing together, forever we'll be,
A testament to love's true harmony.

R. Allure

Contents

CHAPTER 1

INTRODUCTION

In a rapidly changing world, the dynamics of human relationships have undergone a profound transformation. Gone are the days of traditional roles and fixed expectations. In their place, we find a diverse landscape of partnerships, where love, connection, and personal growth take centre stage. "TheyHeal - Uniting Love, Wellness, and the Journey to Wholeness" is an exploration of this new era, a guide that navigates the intricacies of modern relationships while prioritising mental wellness.

The purpose of this book is twofold: to shine a light on the often-unspoken challenges that couples, regardless of their gender or sexual orientation, encounter in today's world, and to provide a roadmap for healing and growth. Here, we delve into the profound interplay between mental health, attachment, and neuroscience within the context of romantic partnerships. Our journey is guided by the belief that understanding these intricacies can lead to more compassionate, resilient, and loving relationships.

In the chapters that follow, we will embark on a quest to discover the secrets of thriving in love, forging deeper connections, and achieving emotional equilibrium. We will explore topics such as emotional suppression, the complexities of attraction, the power of vulnerability, and the dance between femininity, masculinity, and neutrality. Together, we will challenge societal influences and expectations, redefine the roles we play, and embrace the new dynamics of modern relationships.

Join us on this transformative journey as we unite love, wellness, and the path to wholeness. Through self-discovery, compassion, and a commitment to mental health, we aim to illuminate the way towards healthier, happier, and more fulfilling relationships for all.

Before we move into the next chapter it is worth knowing the common challenges in relationships with a focus on mental wellbeing and some interesting facts:

1. Communication Issues: Effective communication is essential for a healthy relationship. Misunderstandings and poor communication can lead to stress and conflict.

Fact: According to research, couples who communicate openly and honestly tend to report higher levels of relationship satisfaction.

2. Trust and Infidelity: Trust is the foundation of any relationship. Betrayal through infidelity can lead to feelings of anger, insecurity, and emotional distress.

Fact: Studies show that rebuilding trust after infidelity is possible, but it requires time, effort, and commitment from both partners.

3. Emotional Suppression: Bottling up emotions or suppressing them can have detrimental effects on mental health. It can lead to increased stress, anxiety, and even depression.

Fact: Research suggests that emotional suppression can negatively impact physical health, including increased risk of heart problems.

4. Attachment Styles: Attachment theory plays a significant role in how individuals form and maintain relationships. Understanding your attachment style can lead to more secure and fulfilling connections.

Fact: There are four main attachment styles: secure, anxious-preoccupied, dismissive-avoidant, and fearful-avoidant, each with distinct characteristics.

5. Stress and Lifestyle: The demands of modern life, including work, family, and responsibilities, can create stress and affect mental wellbeing.

Fact: Chronic stress can lead to a range of health issues, including insomnia, anxiety disorders, and even changes in brain structure.

6. Intimacy and Connection: Maintaining emotional and physical intimacy is crucial in a relationship. The loss of intimacy can lead to feelings of loneliness and dissatisfaction.

Fact: Physical touch, such as hugs and cuddling, releases oxytocin, a hormone associated with bonding and emotional connection.

7. Gender and Societal Expectations: Societal norms and expectations around gender roles and relationships can create tension and conflict.

Fact: Studies show that couples who challenge traditional gender roles and share responsibilities tend to report higher relationship satisfaction.

8. Technology and Distraction: Excessive use of technology, including smartphones and social media, can lead to distraction and decreased quality time together.

Fact: Excessive screen time has been linked to decreased relationship satisfaction and increased feelings of loneliness.

9. Parenting and Family Dynamics: Balancing the demands of parenthood and maintaining a strong partnership can be challenging.

Fact: Research indicates that couples who co-parent effectively and support each other tend to have stronger relationships.

10. Self-Care and Mental Health: Neglecting self-care and mental health can affect one's ability to contribute positively to a relationship.

Fact: Prioritising self-care, including regular exercise and stress reduction techniques, can lead to improved mental health and relationship satisfaction.

Understanding and addressing these challenges while prioritising mental health and emotional wellbeing is key to building and maintaining strong, resilient relationships.

CHAPTER 2

MENTAL HEALTH IN RELATIONSHIPS

In the lavish luxury of love, two souls come together, intertwining their lives, dreams, and destinies. This journey often takes them through breath-taking landscapes of joy and celebration, but it can also lead them down winding paths shrouded in mist and uncertainty. In the modern world, where emotional well-being is paramount, the significance of mental health in sustaining a loving and thriving relationship cannot be overstated. Chapter 2 is a heartfelt exploration of this crucial aspect, delving into the profound influence of mental health within couples and the art of recognising and addressing the unique challenges it presents.

Amidst the laughter, the shared dreams, and the comfort of each other's embrace, lie the complex landscapes of mental health that every couple must navigate. Here, we will embark on a journey to understand the integral role of mental well-being in relationships and learn how to be the gentle guides who illuminate the path to healing and wholeness for ourselves and our partners.

Modern Life, Stress, and Mental Health in Loving Relationships

The modern world, with its relentless pace and ever-increasing demands, has cast a long shadow over our mental well-being. Stress, like an uninvited guest, often finds its way into our lives, affecting us in myriad ways. This isn't a solitary struggle but a shared journey for couples, as the emotional turbulence it brings can cast ripples through even the deepest of bonds.

Consider the scenario where long working hours and the constant hustle led to emotional exhaustion. This exhaustion can manifest as irritability, distance, or even emotional withdrawal within a relationship. What once was a sanctuary of love and support can turn into an arena of unintentional conflict. Stress, if not managed, can breed resentment, misunderstandings, and emotional disconnection.

Moreover, the omnipresence of technology and the digital age can amplify stress in relationships. Couples may find themselves engrossed in their devices, diminishing the quality of their emotional connection. The incessant notifications, social media comparisons, and information overload can breed anxiety and insecurity, affecting one's self-esteem and, by extension, their relationships.

In the pursuit of professional success, individuals might neglect self-care and personal boundaries, sacrificing their mental health on the altar of ambition. This sacrifice often goes unnoticed until it affects the couple dynamic. Burnout, anxiety, and depression can cast shadows over the intimacy, communication, and emotional well-being that relationships thrive on.

However, within the complexities and challenges of modern life, lies the potential for transformation. Couples who acknowledge the impact of stress on their mental health can become allies in the quest for emotional balance. They can work together to establish healthier boundaries, prioritise self-care, and create digital detox routines to strengthen their connection. By nurturing their individual well-being, they can, in turn, breathe vitality into their relationship.

It is time to explore how couples can not only recognise these challenges but also embrace them as opportunities for growth. Together, we shall uncover the secrets of nurturing mental wellness and flourishing love, transcending the stressors of modern life to embark on a journey of wholeness.

Here are some examples of how modern life, stress, and mental health can impact loving relationships along with signs to look for:

1. Work-Life Imbalance: With the increasing demands of careers and the always-on nature of technology, couples may struggle to find time for each other. Signs include constant busyness, difficulty scheduling quality time together, and feelings of neglect.

2. Financial Stress: Money concerns, such as debt, job instability, or strained budgets, can lead to tension in relationships. Signs include frequent arguments about finances, secrecy around money matters, and anxiety about the future.

3. Technology Overuse: Excessive screen time and social media use can reduce face-to-face communication and emotional connection. Signs include distraction during intimate moments, constant scrolling, and feelings of jealousy or insecurity due to online interactions.

4. Mental Health Challenges: Conditions like anxiety, depression, and chronic stress can affect one or both partners in a relationship. Signs include mood swings, social withdrawal, emotional

distance, and changes in behaviour or sleep patterns.

5. Parenting Stress: Raising children can be rewarding but also challenging. Couples may experience stress related to differing parenting styles, lack of sleep, or concerns about their children's well-being. Signs include arguments about parenting, feeling overwhelmed, and difficulty maintaining a united front.

6. Lack of Emotional Intimacy: Stress can lead to emotional withdrawal and a decrease in physical intimacy. Signs include decreased affection, reduced interest in sex, and difficulty expressing emotions.

7. Communication Breakdown: High levels of stress can hinder effective communication, leading to misunderstandings and conflicts. Signs include frequent arguments, avoidance of sensitive topics, and a sense of not being heard or understood.

8. Loss of Connection: Over time, chronic stress and mental health challenges can erode the emotional connection between partners. Signs include a feeling of growing apart, lack of shared

interests, and a sense that the relationship has become routine.

9. Escapism: Some individuals may turn to substances or unhealthy coping mechanisms, such as alcohol or overeating, to deal with stress. Signs include changes in behaviour, secrecy, and neglect of responsibilities.

10. Physical Health Impact: Stress can take a toll on physical health, leading to issues like sleep disturbances, headaches, and fatigue. These physical symptoms can, in turn, affect the quality of the relationship.

It's important to recognise these signs early and address them proactively. Seeking support from a therapist or counsellor, practicing effective communication, and prioritising self-care can help couples navigate the challenges of modern life and maintain a healthy, loving relationship. The above provides an insight; however, as the book progresses, we will delve deeper.

In the meantime, here are some examples of how modern life, stress and mental health issues can play out in relationships.

Sarah and James

Sarah and James, a dynamic couple based in London, have always been on the fast track of modern life. Both thriving in demanding careers, their daily lives are a whirlwind of meetings, deadlines, and social commitments. As they've climbed the corporate ladder, the stress has seeped into their relationship. Long working hours and the pressure to perform at their best have left them with little time for each other. Their once vibrant connection has dwindled, replaced by exhaustion and a sense of neglect. Stress-related irritability and emotional distance have taken a toll on their intimacy, prompting them to re-evaluate their work-life balance.

Maya and Emily

Maya and Emily, a loving couple from New York City, have always celebrated their unique connection. However, the bustling city's relentless pace has affected them deeply. Both women are highly successful professionals, and the competitive nature of their careers has led to increased stress and anxiety. This emotional strain has led to unintended consequences in their relationship. While once open and communicative, they now find it challenging to express their feelings and vulnerability. The stress of meeting societal expectations and striving for perfection has created a barrier between them, affecting their emotional intimacy.

Carlos and Miguel

Carlos and Miguel, a exuberant couple from Barcelona in their 50s, have spent decades navigating the complexities of their relationship. While their love has remained strong, the pressures of modern life have brought unexpected challenges. As they approach retirement, financial concerns have cast a shadow over their golden years. The stress of planning for the future and managing their finances has occasionally led to arguments and emotional distance. They've realised that, to maintain their mental well-being and preserve their love, they must find new ways to communicate and support each other through this late-life transition.

These three diverse couples, spanning different backgrounds, sexual orientations, and locations, demonstrate how the stress of modern life can affect relationships in various ways. Whether it's the demands of high-powered careers, societal expectations, or financial worries, each couple must confront these challenges to protect the love they share. In the chapters ahead, we'll explore how these couples can work together to overcome these obstacles and nurture their mental well-being while strengthening their bonds. Now it is worth moving into attachment theory.

CHAPTER 3

ATTACHMENT THEORY AND RELATIONSHIP DYNAMICS

In the intricate shimmy of human relationships, the concept of attachment theory plays a profound and often unspoken role. Just as celestial bodies are drawn together by the force of gravity, individuals are bound to one another by the invisible threads of attachment styles. These styles, deeply rooted in early experiences and emotional bonds, shape the dynamics of love, trust, and intimacy in romantic partnerships.

This chapter embarks on a journey into the fascinating realm of attachment theory and its profound influence on how we love and relate to our partners. We will delve into the various attachment styles, uncovering their origins and deciphering the complex interplay between attachment and relationship dynamics. More importantly, we will explore strategies that empower individuals and couples to cultivate secure and fulfilling attachments, fostering healthier, more enriching connections with their loved ones.

A Bit About Attachment Theory

Please note there are a lot of really good books that can be read about this, so this section will provide an insight; however, in my opinion, it is worth taking some time to explore how we make and cultivate our attachments and understand the nuances behind them. So, just to elaborate: Attachment theory, initially developed by British psychologist John Bowlby and later expanded upon by Mary Ainsworth, is a psychological framework that examines how early relationships with caregivers influence an individual's emotional and social development, particularly in the context of adult romantic relationships.

Attachment theory posits that individuals develop specific attachment styles based on their early experiences with caregivers. These attachment styles can significantly impact how they approach and engage in adult relationships. There are four primary attachment styles:

1. Secure Attachment: People with secure attachment styles tend to have positive views of themselves and their partners. They are comfortable with intimacy and independence, value open communication, and can navigate conflicts effectively. Securely attached individuals typically had caregivers who were responsive and

consistently met their emotional needs during childhood.

2. Anxious-Preoccupied Attachment: Individuals with this attachment style often seek high levels of closeness and reassurance in relationships. They may worry about their partner's availability and fear abandonment. Anxious-preoccupied individuals often had inconsistent caregiving during childhood, with caregivers who were sometimes responsive and sometimes not.

3. Dismissive-Avoidant Attachment: Those with a dismissive-avoidant attachment style tend to prioritise independence and self-sufficiency. They may be uncomfortable with emotional intimacy and may downplay the importance of close relationships. This attachment style often develops when caregivers are emotionally distant or unresponsive during childhood.

4. Fearful-Avoidant (Disorganised) Attachment: People with fearful-avoidant attachment styles often have conflicting desires for both closeness and distance in relationships. They may have experienced trauma or unpredictable caregiving during childhood, leading to a sense of fear and uncertainty in adult relationships.

Attachment styles are not fixed but can evolve over time based on new relationship experiences and personal growth. Understanding your own attachment style and that of your partner can be instrumental in improving communication, resolving conflicts, and fostering a more secure and satisfying romantic relationship. It provides valuable insights into how individuals express love, navigate intimacy, and cope with challenges in relationships.

Discovering your attachment style and embracing it can be a valuable journey towards understanding yourself and improving your relationships.

Here's how to go about it:

1. Self-Reflection:

- Start by examining your own emotional responses and behaviours in relationships. Think about how you typically react when you or your partner faces challenges or conflicts.
- Consider your childhood experiences and early relationships with caregivers. Were they consistently responsive and nurturing, or did you experience inconsistency or neglect?

2. Self-Assessment:

- Various self-assessment tools, quizzes, and
  questionnaires are available online and in self-
  help books that can help you identify your
  attachment style. These quizzes often present
  scenarios and ask you to choose the response
  that best describes your feelings and
  behaviours.

3. Seek Professional Help:

- If you find it challenging to identify your
  attachment style or have concerns about its
  impact on your mental health or relationships,
  consider consulting a therapist or counsellor.
  They can provide guidance, assessment, and
  therapy tailored to your specific needs.

4. Observe Patterns:

- Pay attention to recurring patterns in your
  relationships. Do you often experience the
  same challenges or conflicts? Are there
  specific triggers that cause emotional
  reactions?
- Reflect on your emotional responses to
  closeness, intimacy, and independence in your
  relationships.

5. Embrace Your Style:

- Once you identify your attachment style,
  remember that it's not inherently good or bad.
  It's simply a way of understanding your
  emotional needs and how you relate to others.
- Embrace your attachment style with self-
  compassion. Understand that it has developed
  based on your life experiences, and it's a part
  of who you are.

6. Communication and Growth:

- Share your attachment style with your partner
  if you're in a relationship. Open, honest
  communication can help both of you
  understand each other better.
- Work on personal growth and self-awareness.
  Consider therapy or self-help resources to
  address any challenges related to your
  attachment style.

7. Seek Secure Relationships:

- If you have an insecure attachment style, aim
  to create secure and supportive relationships.
  Surround yourself with people who respect
  your boundaries and emotional needs.

- Cultivate relationships with those who can provide emotional support and consistency.

Remember that attachment styles are not static; they can evolve and change over time with self-awareness and effort. Embracing your attachment style is a step towards healthier and more fulfilling relationships, as it allows you to better understand and meet your emotional needs while navigating the complexities of human connection.

Cultivating mental health in a relationship involves understanding attachment styles and using this knowledge to create a supportive and secure emotional environment. Here are some key insights and tips:

1. Recognise Your Attachment Style:

- Understanding your own attachment style is the first step. Be honest with yourself about your tendencies and emotional responses in relationships.

2. Communicate Openly:

- Share your attachment style and insights with your partner. Encourage open and non-judgmental conversations about attachment and emotional needs.
- Discuss how your attachment styles may interact and affect your relationship dynamics.

3. Develop Self-Awareness:

- Cultivate self-awareness regarding your emotional triggers and responses. Identify moments when your attachment style may be influencing your reactions.
- Reflect on your past experiences and how they may have shaped your attachment style.

4. Empathy and Understanding:

- Recognise that your partner also has an attachment style, and it may differ from yours. Practice empathy and seek to understand their needs and emotional responses.
- Be patient and compassionate with each other's vulnerabilities and insecurities.

5. Create a Secure Base:

- Aim to provide a secure and supportive base for each other. Foster a sense of safety, trust, and reliability in your relationship.
- Offer emotional support during challenging times and celebrate each other's successes.

6. Address Insecurities:

- If you or your partner have an insecure attachment style, be willing to address insecurities and work on healing together.
- Seek therapy or counselling if needed to explore and address attachment-related issues.

7. Set Healthy Boundaries:

- Establish and communicate clear boundaries within the relationship. Respect each other's individuality and personal space.
- Healthy boundaries can help create a sense of safety and predictability.

8. Seek Growth and Change:

- Be open to personal growth and change. Attachment styles can evolve with self-awareness and effort.
- Encourage each other to work on any unhealthy attachment patterns or behaviours.

9. Prioritise Self-Care:

-   Individual mental health is the foundation for a healthy relationship. Prioritise self-care, including activities and practices that promote your well-being.
-   Encourage your partner to engage in self-care as well.

10. Seek Professional Help:

-   If you find that attachment-related issues are significantly impacting your relationship or mental health, consider seeking the assistance of a therapist or counsellor.
-   Professional guidance can provide tools and strategies to address attachment challenges effectively.

Remember that cultivating mental health in a relationship is an ongoing process. It requires effort, understanding, and a willingness to support each other's emotional well-being. By embracing attachment styles and using them as a framework for understanding your relationship dynamics, you can create a healthier, more fulfilling partnership based on trust, security, and love.

What you may find fascinating is that attachment styles are closely linked to neuroscience and brain wiring, particularly in how individuals process emotions and form connections in relationships. Here's how attachment styles relate to neuroscience and brain functioning:

1. Brain Wiring and Attachment Styles:

- Attachment styles are thought to have roots in early childhood experiences, especially interactions with caregivers. These early experiences can shape the brain's neural pathways and structures related to emotion regulation and social bonding.

2. Emotional Regulation:

- Neuroscience research has shown that individuals with secure attachment styles tend to have well-developed emotion regulation systems. Their brains are better equipped to handle stress and emotional challenges.
- In contrast, those with insecure attachment styles may exhibit differences in the brain's emotional processing regions, making it more challenging to regulate emotions effectively.

3. Neural Responses to Attachment-Related Cues:

- Studies using brain imaging techniques like fMRI have demonstrated that attachment-related cues, such as images of loved ones or emotionally charged scenarios, can elicit distinct neural responses.
- For example, individuals with anxious attachment styles may show heightened activation in brain regions associated with worry and anxiety when faced with attachment-related stressors.

4. Mirror Neurons and Social Bonding:

- Mirror neurons, specialised cells in the brain, play a role in social bonding and empathy. They allow individuals to mimic and understand the emotions and actions of others.
- In secure attachments, mirror neurons may facilitate positive social interactions, empathy, and emotional attunement between partners. Conversely, insecure attachments can affect how mirror neurons function in relationships.

5. Hormonal Regulation:

- Attachment styles can influence the release of stress hormones, such as cortisol. Securely attached individuals may experience less stress and cortisol reactivity in challenging relationship situations.
- Insecure attachment styles, on the other hand, may be associated with heightened stress responses, affecting both mental and physical health.

6. The Role of Early Experiences:

- Early caregiving experiences, including responsive parenting and emotional attunement, can have a lasting impact on brain development. Secure attachments foster healthy brain functioning and emotional well-being.
- Traumatic or neglectful early experiences can lead to alterations in the brain's stress response systems, potentially contributing to later attachment challenges.

7. Neuroplasticity and Change:

-   The brain's capacity for neuroplasticity means that attachment styles can evolve over time. Therapeutic interventions, self-awareness, and personal growth efforts can reshape neural pathways and promote more secure attachments.

Understanding the neuroscience of attachment styles can offer valuable insights into relationship dynamics and emotional regulation. It highlights the brain's adaptability and the potential for positive changes through self-awareness and intentional efforts to foster secure attachments and healthy relationships. This leads nicely into the next chapter… Yipeee!

CHAPTER 4

THE NEUROSCIENCE OF LOVE

Love is a complex and profound human experience, one that has captured the imaginations of poets, artists, and scientists alike for centuries. Beyond its emotional depth, love is also a phenomenon rooted in the intricate workings of the human brain. In this chapter, we delve into the captivating world of the neuroscience of love, exploring how the brain processes love, attraction, and the deep emotional connections that bind us.

Within the intricate neural networks of our brains, love finds its home, guiding our behaviours, thoughts, and emotions. We'll uncover the neural pathways that govern romantic attraction, the role of mirror neurons in fostering empathy and emotional bonding, and the remarkable ways in which our brains enable us to experience the most profound of human emotions. Join us as we embark on a journey through the terrain of the heart and mind, unlocking the secrets of love's neurological embrace.

The Neuroscience of Love: Deciphering the Brain's Dance of Attraction

At the heart of the intricate symphony of human emotions, love takes centre stage. Whether it's the exhilaration of a budding romance, the warmth of familial bonds, or the enduring affection of long-term partnerships, love paints the canvas of our lives with vibrant hues. Yet, beneath the surface of these emotional masterpieces lies a fascinating and complex neurological landscape. In this chapter, we embark on a journey through the brain's intricate pathways, unravelling the mysteries of how it processes love, attraction, and the profound emotional connections that define our existence.

Within the neural networks of our brain, love manifests as a captivating interplay of chemistry and emotion. From the initial spark of attraction to the deep-seated bonds of attachment, our brain orchestrates this intricate dance. Neurotransmitters like dopamine and oxytocin surge during moments of connection and intimacy, rewarding us with pleasure and fostering emotional attachment. But love's neural story doesn't end there. We explore the brain regions responsible for processing the multifaceted facets of love, from the passionate fires of romantic attraction in the ventral tegmental area to the soothing embrace of maternal love in the brain's caregiving networks.

The brain regions responsible for processing different facets of love play a crucial role in shaping our relationships and influencing our mental health and well-being.

1. Ventral Tegmental Area (VTA): This region is often associated with the passionate fires of romantic attraction. It's a part of the brain's reward system and releases the neurotransmitter dopamine during moments of pleasure and attraction. When you're in love or attracted to someone, your VTA is actively engaged, creating feelings of euphoria and excitement. In the context of relationships, the VTA's activity fosters the initial stages of romance and intense connection. This passionate aspect of love can contribute to feelings of happiness and fulfilment in a relationship, positively impacting mental well-being.

2. Cingulate Cortex and Insula: These brain regions are involved in processing empathy and emotional pain. They enable us to understand and resonate with the emotions of our loved ones. When your partner is going through a difficult time, these regions help you empathise and provide support. In healthy relationships, the ability to empathise and offer emotional support is essential for maintaining mental well-being. It fosters a sense of closeness and emotional safety.

3. Oxytocin Release: The release of oxytocin, often referred to as the "love hormone" or "cuddle hormone," plays a significant role in maternal love and caregiving networks. It's released during moments of bonding, such as hugging, cuddling, or when a mother interacts with her child. Oxytocin promotes feelings of trust, bonding, and emotional connection. In relationships, this hormone strengthens the emotional attachment between partners. A strong emotional bond can provide a sense of security and reduce stress, contributing to improved mental health and well-being.

In summary, these brain regions and their associated functions influence our emotional experiences in relationships. The passion of romantic attraction, the ability to empathise, and the nurturing aspect of love all contribute to our mental well-being within relationships. Positive emotional experiences, emotional support, and a strong sense of connection foster mental health and contribute to overall relationship satisfaction. Understanding the neural basis of these experiences can help individuals navigate their relationships with greater awareness and appreciation for the brain's role in matters of the heart.

Fascinatingly, our brain is equipped with mirror neurons, specialised cells that enable us to empathise and emotionally synchronise with our loved ones. These neurons allow us to resonate with the emotions of others, creating a profound sense of connection. As we delve into the depths of love's neuroscience, we'll uncover how mirror neurons play a pivotal role in fostering empathy and emotional bonding, reinforcing the idea that love is a fundamental force that shapes our neural architecture. Throughout this exploration, we'll unearth captivating facts and insights that shed light on the neural underpinnings of love, transforming our understanding of this most cherished of human experiences.

Mirror neurons are remarkable cells in our brain that have profound implications for our relationships, healing, and mental health:

1. The Empathy Engine: Mirror neurons act as the brain's "empathy engine." When we observe someone experiencing an emotion, these neurons fire as if we were experiencing that emotion ourselves. This mechanism allows us to deeply connect with the emotions of our loved ones. For example, when your partner is joyful, mirror neurons help you share in their happiness, enhancing your emotional bond.

2. Building Emotional Bridges: Mirror neurons bridge the emotional gap between individuals. They enable us to synchronise emotionally, creating a powerful sense of connection. In relationships, this synchronisation can lead to mutual understanding and emotional support. It's as if our brains are wired to share in each other's emotional experiences.

3. Strengthening Bonds: Mirror neurons are integral to the bonding process. When a parent and child gaze into each other's eyes, mirror neurons facilitate this emotional connection. In romantic relationships, shared emotional experiences, such as laughter or shared moments of vulnerability, can deepen the emotional bond between partners.

4. Healing Through Connection: The ability of mirror neurons to foster empathy and connection has therapeutic implications. In therapy settings, the therapist's empathy and attunement can help clients heal from emotional wounds. The empathetic connection formed through mirror neurons can create a safe space for emotional exploration and healing.

5. Mental Health Benefits: Strong emotional bonds and a sense of connection, fostered by mirror neurons, contribute to improved mental health. Feeling understood, supported, and emotionally connected can reduce stress, anxiety, and depression. In romantic relationships, these bonds can be a source of emotional resilience.

In summary, mirror neurons play a pivotal role in the neural underpinnings of love, empathy, and emotional connection. They facilitate synchronisation of emotions and strengthen the bonds between individuals. This neural mechanism not only enriches our relationships but also has therapeutic potential, aiding in emotional healing and contributing to enhanced mental well-being. Understanding the role of mirror neurons reinforces the idea that love is a fundamental force shaping our neural architecture and emotional experiences.

Harnessing the power of mirror neurons can significantly benefit our relationships, healing processes, and mental health. Here are some ways to utilise these remarkable cells for your well-being:

1. Enhance Empathy: Cultivate empathy by actively practicing it in your relationships. Listen attentively to your loved ones, trying to understand their feelings and perspectives. When you genuinely empathise, your mirror neurons kick in, strengthening emotional connections and building trust.

2. Validation: Use mirror neurons to validate others' emotions. Acknowledging and validating someone's feelings can help them feel heard and understood, promoting emotional healing. Phrases like "I can see that you're feeling upset, and it's okay to feel that way" show empathy and validation.

3. Shared Activities: Engage in shared activities that elicit positive emotions together. Whether it's enjoying a favourite meal, watching a funny movie, or practicing a hobby, shared experiences can strengthen emotional bonds by activating mirror neurons in response to shared emotions.

4. Seek Emotional Support: In times of need, reach out to trusted friends, family, or therapists who can provide emotional support. The act of sharing your feelings and receiving empathy from others can activate mirror neurons, providing comfort and healing.

5. Practice Mindfulness: Mindfulness meditation can enhance your awareness of your own emotions and those of others. This practice can strengthen your ability to resonate with the emotions of loved ones and respond empathetically.

6. Therapeutic Relationships: In therapy, choose a therapist with whom you feel a strong emotional connection. The empathetic bond formed with a therapist can facilitate healing, as the therapist's mirror neurons resonate with your emotional experiences.

7. Self-Compassion: Extend the empathetic qualities of mirror neurons to yourself. Practice self-compassion by acknowledging your own emotions and treating yourself with kindness and understanding, especially during challenging times.

8. Positive Communication: Use empathetic and validating language in your conversations. Express your understanding of the other person's feelings, even if you don't necessarily agree with their perspective. This promotes open, healthy communication.

9. Strengthen Relationships: In romantic partnerships, prioritise emotional connection. Share vulnerable moments, celebrate joys together, and create a safe space for each other's emotions. These actions engage mirror neurons and strengthen the emotional bond.

10. Community Support: Seek support from like-minded communities or support groups where you can connect with individuals who share similar experiences. Sharing stories and emotions within a supportive community can foster healing and a sense of belonging.

By consciously incorporating these practices into your life, you can leverage the power of mirror neurons to deepen your relationships, facilitate emotional healing, and enhance your overall mental health and well-being.

Why not have a play? You can engage with your mirror neurons and recognise when they are at play through various activities and observations:

1. Practice Empathetic Listening: When you engage in a conversation with someone, especially during emotional moments, try to actively listen. Put yourself in their shoes and genuinely try to understand their perspective. Mirror neurons are at work when you feel an emotional resonance with the speaker, experiencing a similar emotion.

2. Observe Nonverbal Cues: Pay attention to nonverbal cues during interactions. Mirror neurons are responsible for mirroring facial expressions, body language, and gestures. If you find yourself naturally mimicking these cues, it's a sign that your mirror neurons are active.

3. Engage in Role-Playing: Role-playing exercises with a partner or in group settings can activate mirror neurons. By stepping into another person's role, you experience their emotions and reactions, enhancing your empathetic abilities.

4. Read Fiction and Watch Movies: When you read a novel or watch a movie, you often become

emotionally invested in the characters' experiences. This is because mirror neurons simulate the characters' emotions in your brain, allowing you to feel what they feel.

5. Volunteer and Help Others: Engaging in volunteer work or acts of kindness activates mirror neurons. When you help someone in need and witness their gratitude or happiness, your mirror neurons create a sense of connection and fulfilment.

6. Yoga and Meditation: Mindfulness practices like yoga and meditation can increase your awareness of emotional states. These techniques help you observe your own emotions and reactions, fostering empathy for yourself and others.

7. Practice Self-Compassion: Extend empathy to yourself by practicing self-compassion. Treat yourself with the same kindness and understanding you offer to others, activating mirror neurons in self-reflection.

8. Reflect on Empathetic Moments: After engaging in empathetic interactions, take some time to reflect on the emotions you experienced. Recognise how mirror neurons played a role in creating a sense of connection and understanding.

By incorporating these practices into your daily life, you can become more attuned to your mirror neurons and their role in enhancing empathy, connection, and emotional support in your relationships.

Here are three heart-warming stories of couples from diverse backgrounds and orientations who used mirror neuron techniques to enhance their relationships and well-being:

Millie and Sarah

Millie and Sarah, a loving couple of ladies in their mid-30s, faced a significant challenge when Sarah's mother fell seriously ill. The stress and emotional toll were overwhelming. Millie and Sarah turned to mirror neuron techniques to navigate this difficult time. They practiced empathetic listening, taking turns sharing their concerns and fears while actively mirroring each other's emotions. This deepened their emotional connection, helping them support each other effectively.

Outcome: Millie and Sarah emerged from this challenging period with a stronger bond. By using mirror neurons to empathise with each other's worries, they not only provided emotional support but also deepened their own connection.

Antonio and Magik

Antonio and Magik, a loving couple of chaps in their 50s, were approaching their 30th anniversary. Over the years, they faced various life challenges together, including career changes and health issues. To strengthen their relationship, they practiced mindfulness meditation and mirror neuron techniques. This allowed them to share their emotions openly, enhancing their understanding of each other's needs and desires.

Outcome: Antonio and Magik relationship grew even more resilient. By using mirror neurons and mindfulness, they created a space for vulnerability and emotional support. Their enduring love continued to thrive.

Emma and Chris

Emma and Chris, a heterosexual couple in their 40s, found themselves stuck in a cycle of misunderstanding and frustration. They decided to seek relationship therapy, where they learned about mirror neurons and empathetic communication. They practiced active listening and validation, allowing each other to express their feelings without judgment. This transformed their interactions and reignited their connection.

Outcome: Emma and Chris discovered newfound empathy in their relationship. By embracing mirror neuron techniques, they broke free from their communication barriers. Their love flourished, and they found deeper happiness in their marriage.

These stories illustrate the power of mirror neurons to enhance empathy, promote emotional support, and strengthen relationships, regardless of gender or orientation. Through intentional practice and a commitment to emotional connection, couples can navigate life's challenges and find lasting happiness together.

CHAPTER 5

BREAKING THE ILLUSION OF PROJECTION

In the intricate dance of relationships, our emotions often take the lead, guiding our steps through the intricate choreography of love, conflict, and connection. Yet, in this delicate performance, there is a hidden player—an enigmatic figure known as projection. Much like a shadow cast by unseen forces, projection has the power to distort the truth, casting our own unresolved emotions onto the stage of our relationships. It is a phenomenon as old as humanity itself but understanding it can lead to profound transformation.

In this chapter, we delve into the art of breaking the illusion of projection. We explore how projection manifests in our interactions, creating misunderstandings and conflicts. By shining a light on this psychological phenomenon, we empower ourselves with the tools to become more self-aware and regain control over our emotional narratives. Through self-reflection and insightful techniques, we step out of the shadows and into the light of clarity, allowing our relationships to flourish with authenticity and understanding.

Here's an elaboration on projection in relationships and its connection to mental health:

Projection in Relationships: Unveiling the Shadows

Projection is a psychological defence mechanism where individuals attribute their own thoughts, feelings, or characteristics onto others. It's as if we take aspects of ourselves that we find uncomfortable or unacceptable and unconsciously project them onto our partners or those close to us. This phenomenon can subtly infiltrate our interactions, shaping the dynamics of our relationships, and often, it goes unnoticed.

In relationships, projection can manifest in various ways:

1. Blame and Criticism: When we find ourselves frequently blaming or criticising our partner for things that seem irrational or disproportionate to the situation, it may be an indication of projection. We might be projecting our own insecurities or fears onto our partner, seeing in them what we don't want to acknowledge within ourselves.

2. Idealisation and Devaluation: Projection can also lead to idealising our partner, attributing qualities to them that we admire but may not fully recognise in ourselves. Conversely, it can result in devaluation, where we perceive our partner as embodying the qualities we dislike about ourselves.

3. Transference: In therapeutic terms, transference is a form of projection that occurs when feelings and attitudes towards significant figures from our past are unconsciously transferred onto our current relationships. This can impact how we perceive and react to our partner.

Projection and Mental Health: The Hidden Impact

Projection isn't just a quirk of the mind; it can have profound implications for mental health. When we project our unresolved emotions or unacknowledged parts of ourselves onto others, we avoid facing these issues directly. Over time, this avoidance can lead to heightened stress, anxiety, and emotional turmoil. It can also erode the trust and intimacy in our relationships, making it challenging to cultivate genuine connections.

Recognising Projection for Mental Health and Relationship Growth

Understanding projection is a vital step in improving mental health and enhancing relationships. It begins with self-awareness. By developing a deeper understanding of our own emotions, triggers, and insecurities, we can start to recognise when we're projecting onto others. This self-awareness allows us to take responsibility for our feelings and behaviours, rather than attributing them to someone else.

Breaking the illusion of projection requires patience, self-reflection, and open communication in relationships. It's about having honest conversations with our partners and learning to differentiate between our own emotions and those we might be projecting onto them. As we shed light on the shadows of projection, we pave the way for healthier relationships and improved mental well-being.

Understanding triggers and learning to differentiate between what is yours and what belongs to the circumstances or others is crucial for mental health and healthy relationships. Here's an explanation of this concept and how it applies:

Navigating Triggers and Differentiating Ownership: A Path to Emotional Well-Being

1. Identifying Triggers: Triggers are events, situations, or behaviours that cause emotional reactions. These reactions can be intense and may stem from past experiences, fears, or unresolved issues. Recognising your triggers is the first step in gaining control over your emotional responses.

2. Self-Awareness: When you notice a strong emotional reaction, pause and reflect. Ask yourself whether this reaction is proportionate to the current situation. Is it possible that the intensity of your feelings is connected to something deeper from your past?

3. Own Your Emotions: Take responsibility for your emotions, regardless of their source. Emotions are valid and real experiences, but they may not always be directly linked to the present moment. Acknowledging your feelings and understanding that they are yours is an essential part of emotional intelligence.

4. External Circumstances: Sometimes, situations or events are genuinely challenging, and your emotional response is a natural reaction to external circumstances. In such cases, it's crucial to distinguish between what is a reasonable reaction to a difficult situation and what might be an overreaction based on personal triggers.

5. Communicate Openly: If you're in a relationship, communicate openly with your partner about your triggers and emotional responses. Let them know when you're struggling and when you need support. Encourage your partner to do the same. This transparency fosters empathy and understanding.

6. Self-Care: Take care of your mental and emotional well-being. Engage in self-care practices that help you manage your triggers and maintain emotional balance. This might include mindfulness, meditation, journaling, or seeking professional help when needed.

7. Support and Boundaries: Establish clear boundaries in your relationships. Communicate your needs and limits to your partner, and respect theirs as well. Knowing when to seek support from your partner and when to address your emotions independently is essential.

8. Seek Context: When you encounter emotional triggers, seek to understand the context. Is there a pattern or theme in your triggers? Are they related to specific past experiences or traumas? Exploring the context can provide valuable insights into your emotional landscape.

9. Healing and Growth: If your triggers are deeply rooted in past traumas or unresolved issues, consider therapy or counseling to address these underlying challenges. Healing and personal growth can lead to reduced reactivity to triggers and improved mental health.

10. Empathy for Others: Just as you seek to understand your triggers, extend empathy to others in your relationships. Recognise that they may also have triggers and emotional reactions influenced by their past experiences. Cultivating empathy can foster greater compassion and connection.

Differentiating between what is yours and what belongs to external circumstances or others is a skill that requires practice and self-awareness. It allows you to respond to challenging situations more effectively and maintain healthier relationships while prioritising your mental well-being.

Moving from blame to responsibility is a crucial step in improving mental health and enhancing relationships. Here's a good approach on how to make this shift and use it as an opportunity for growth:

Moving from Blame to Responsibility: A Path to Mental Health and Relationship Enhancement

1. Self-Reflection: Begin by turning your attention inward. Take time to reflect on your own thoughts, feelings, and behaviours. Ask yourself why you might be feeling the way you do and whether there are any patterns or triggers you've noticed in your reactions.

2. Identifying Blame: Recognise moments when you tend to blame others for your emotions or problems. This might involve pointing fingers at your partner for causing certain feelings or circumstances. Awareness is the first step in making a change.

3. Practice Self-Compassion: Understand that it's human to experience a range of emotions, including frustration, anger, and sadness. Instead of judging yourself for feeling these emotions, practice self-compassion. Treat yourself with the same kindness and understanding you would offer to a friend facing similar challenges.

4. Explore Vulnerability: Often, blame serves as a defence mechanism to protect our vulnerability. We might blame others as a way to shield ourselves from feelings of inadequacy or fear. By acknowledging and embracing your vulnerability, you can create space for authentic connection and growth.

5. Take Responsibility: Instead of blaming, shift your perspective to take responsibility for your own emotions and reactions. This doesn't mean dismissing your feelings but recognising that they are your own. Phrases like "I feel..." or "I am experiencing..." can help you express your emotions without attributing them to someone else.

6. Open Communication: Engage in open and honest communication with your partner. Share your thoughts and emotions, emphasising that you take responsibility for them. Encourage your partner to do the same. This creates a safe space for vulnerability and understanding.

7. Seek Solutions: Once you've taken responsibility for your feelings, work together with your partner to find solutions or compromises that benefit both of you. This collaborative approach fosters mutual respect and strengthens your relationship.

8. Learn and Grow: Viewing challenges as opportunities for personal and relational growth can be empowering. Consider therapy or counseling as a valuable resource to explore deeper emotional issues and develop healthier coping strategies.

9. Practice Patience: Changing your approach to blame takes time and practice. Be patient with yourself and your partner as you both navigate this shift. Celebrate small victories and learn from setbacks.

10. Reap the Benefits: By embracing responsibility, you not only improve your mental health but also enhance the quality of your relationships. You'll find greater emotional intimacy, trust, and a sense of empowerment in taking charge of your own well-being.

Remember that this transition is a journey, and it's okay to seek support along the way. Whether through self-help resources, therapy, or couples counseling, the process of moving from blame to responsibility can lead to a more fulfilling and mentally healthy life.

CHAPTER 6

BUILDING ATTRACTION AND CONNECTION

In the sophisticated salsa of human relationships, attraction and connection are the heartbeats that infuse vitality and warmth into our partnerships. They are the invisible threads that weave emotional tapestries of intimacy and belonging. Yet, in the context of modern life's complexities, fostering and maintaining these essential elements can sometimes feel like navigating uncharted waters. In this chapter, we dive deep into the art of building attraction and connection, exploring the factors that underpin these core elements of love and affection.

Attraction, in its multifaceted forms, transcends the realm of mere physical allure. We'll unravel the intricate interplay of factors that contribute to attraction, discovering that it is not solely skin deep, but a rich tapestry woven with shared values, interests, and emotional resonance. As we delve into the dynamics of attraction, we'll also shine a light on the role of self-esteem and self-worth in nurturing healthy connections.

Moreover, we'll explore the avenues that lead to emotional and physical intimacy within relationships. We'll uncover the importance of vulnerability, open communication, and empathy in building the bridges that span the chasm between two souls. We'll also delve into the intricacies of physical connection, highlighting its significance in fortifying the emotional bonds that underpin successful and fulfilling relationships. As we embark on this journey of discovery, we'll unveil how nurturing attraction and connection within couples not only fosters emotional well-being but also catalyses mental healing and supports positive mental states. It's an exploration of love's alchemy and its profound impact on the wellness of mind, body, and soul.

With that in mind, let's delve into some fascinating facts about factors contributing to attraction and intimacy:

1. The Power of Laughter:

- Laughter truly is universal. Studies have shown that shared laughter releases endorphins, the body's natural feel-good chemicals. This not only fosters a sense of bonding but also contributes to physical attraction.
- International Fact: In Japan, there's a popular form of therapy called "laughter yoga," where people gather to laugh heartily together, promoting emotional bonding and reducing stress.

2. The Scent of Attraction:

- Our sense of smell plays a significant role in attraction. Pheromones, chemical compounds released by our bodies, can influence sexual attraction and bonding.
- International Fact: In some Middle Eastern cultures, it's customary for brides and grooms to exchange scents before the wedding, symbolising the desire for lasting attraction.

3. The Role of Music:

- Sharing musical preferences can enhance emotional connection. Couples who enjoy similar music often report higher levels of satisfaction in their relationships.
- International Fact: In India, classical music has been used for centuries to enhance the romantic mood during courtship and intimacy.

4. Cultural Influences on Attraction:

- Cultural backgrounds can influence what individuals find attractive. For example, in some cultures, fair skin is considered more attractive, while in others, darker skin tones are favoured.
- International Fact: In South Korea, the "V-line" face shape (a slim and tapered jawline) has been considered attractive, leading to the popularity of cosmetic procedures to achieve it.

5. The Importance of Touch:

- Physical touch, such as hugging and holding hands, releases oxytocin, often referred to as the "love hormone." It strengthens emotional bonds and increases feelings of intimacy.
- International Fact: In many African cultures, communal bathing is a tradition that promotes

closeness and bonding among family and
community members.

6. Shared Adventures:

-    Engaging in exciting or novel activities together
     can stimulate attraction. The adrenaline rush
     from shared adventures can create a sense of
     excitement and bonding.
-    International Fact: In New Zealand, couples
     often bond over outdoor adventures like
     bungee jumping or exploring the country's
     stunning landscapes.

These facts highlight the diversity and universality
of attraction and intimacy factors across different
cultures and regions. Understanding these
elements can help couples cultivate deeper
connections and enhance their relationships,
ultimately contributing to their mental well-being
and happiness.

Time to explore how to nurture emotional and physical connection in relationships with three enjoyable techniques:

1. Nature's Embrace:

- Spend quality time together in nature. Whether it's a leisurely hike, a serene picnic by the lake, or a relaxing day at the beach, nature offers a wonderful backdrop for emotional connection.
- Technique: Choose a natural setting that resonates with both of you. As you immerse yourselves in the beauty of the outdoors, take moments to express your thoughts, feelings, and gratitude for each other. Share stories, laughter, and even dreams while appreciating the tranquillity of nature.

2. Laughter Yoga and Playful Connection:

- Laughter is a powerful tool for building emotional bonds. Consider joining a laughter yoga class or simply engage in playful activities at home.
- Technique: Try a playful game of Twister together. This classic game involves physical closeness and laughter as you twist and turn to match the coloured dots. The laughter and physical contact can strengthen your connection and create joyful memories.

3. Dance of the Elements:

- Connect with the elements by experiencing the dance of wind, fire, water, and earth. This unique bonding activity fosters a sense of unity with nature and each other.
- Technique: Choose an element to explore together. For instance, if you select water, find a tranquil spot by a river or waterfall. Close your eyes, feel the coolness of the water, and share your emotions and thoughts inspired by this element. Allow the conversation to flow naturally, deepening your emotional connection.

These techniques aim to create moments of joy, laughter, and deep connection between partners. They encourage open communication, vulnerability, and shared experiences that can enhance emotional and physical intimacy. By nurturing your bond in these creative ways, you can strengthen your relationship, promote mental well-being, and cultivate lasting love.

Here are three stories of diverse couples who engaged in the mentioned exercises and the outcomes they experienced:

Nature's Embrace - Sarah and Mia

Sarah and Mia decided to take a weekend getaway to a peaceful cabin in the Canadian Rockies. Surrounded by pristine nature, they embarked on their Nature's Embrace journey. While sitting by the lakeside, Sarah shared her dreams of traveling the world and Mia talked about her desire to explore art. This deep, nature-inspired conversation led to greater emotional intimacy and the realisation that they both supported each other's ambitions. They left the cabin with a newfound sense of connection and determination to pursue their dreams together, their mental well-being bolstered by their strong emotional bond.

Laughter Yoga and Playful Connection - John and Emily

John and Emily, both juggling demanding careers and parenting, decided to rekindle their connection through laughter. They joined a laughter yoga class together, initially feeling a bit self-conscious. As they engaged in the laughter exercises and saw each other's joyful, uninhibited side, their laughter became genuine. Back home, they introduced humour into their daily lives, often bursting into spontaneous fits of laughter. The atmosphere of playfulness reinvigorated their relationship, reduced stress, and strengthened their emotional connection. Their evenings now ended with shared laughter, making their mental well-being and relationship thrive.

Dance of the Elements - Javier and Mateo

Javier and Mateo decided to explore the Dance of the Elements at a picturesque coastal spot. They chose the element of fire, symbolising passion and energy. They watched the sunset, feeling the warmth of the sun on their skin. Mateo shared his dreams of starting a business, and Javier revealed his longing to travel the world. As they talked, they lit a small bonfire. The crackling flames seemed to mirror their shared enthusiasm and desires. This experience allowed them to be vulnerable with each other, fostering a deeper emotional connection. They left with a sense of unity and newfound strength in their relationship, knowing that their dreams could be achieved together.

These stories showcase how diverse couples can use creative techniques to nurture emotional and physical connections, leading to improved mental well-being and stronger relationships. Each couple found their unique path to deeper intimacy and shared happiness.

Building attraction and connection in a relationship can have profound positive effects on mental health and overall well-being. Here are some valuable insights:

1. Reduced Stress Levels: Engaging in activities that nurture emotional and physical connection, such as laughter or intimate conversations, can trigger the release of endorphins, the body's natural stress-relievers. This can significantly reduce stress levels, promoting mental well-being.

2. Enhanced Emotional Bond: Activities that foster attraction and connection create opportunities for deeper emotional intimacy. Sharing dreams, desires, and vulnerabilities allows couples to connect on a more profound level, which can lead to increased feelings of security and happiness.

3. Improved Communication: Building attraction and connection often involves open and honest communication. These exercises encourage couples to express themselves and actively listen to their partner's thoughts and feelings. This improved communication can reduce misunderstandings and conflicts, contributing to better mental health.

4. Boosted Confidence: Engaging in activities that strengthen emotional bonds can boost self-esteem and self-confidence. Feeling valued and desired by your partner can enhance your overall sense of self-worth, positively impacting mental well-being.

5. Enhanced Positive Emotions: Laughter, playfulness, and shared experiences generate positive emotions. These positive emotions can counteract feelings of sadness or anxiety, contributing to a more optimistic outlook on life.

6. Greater Resilience: Couples who actively work on building attraction and connection often develop greater resilience in the face of challenges. A strong emotional bond can provide a solid foundation for overcoming life's obstacles, making individuals more mentally resilient.

7. Improved Relationship Satisfaction: Ultimately, these activities lead to increased relationship satisfaction. When individuals feel more connected to their partner and experience a deeper sense of attraction, they are more likely to report higher levels of overall life satisfaction and better mental health.

8. Stress Buffer: A strong emotional connection acts as a buffer against the negative effects of stress. Couples who feel deeply connected tend to handle stressors more effectively, which can prevent the detrimental impact of chronic stress on mental health.

In summary, nurturing attraction and connection in a relationship not only strengthens the partnership but also provides a wealth of mental health benefits. These activities promote emotional well-being, reduce stress, and contribute to overall life satisfaction, enhancing both individual and collective mental health.

CHAPTER 7

SUCCESSFUL RELATIONSHIPS

In the diversity of human encounters, few pursuits are as cherished and sought after as that of a successful and fulfilling relationship. Yet, the very essence of success in such an endeavour often eludes precise definition, for love, like life itself, is an ever-evolving journey, a dance of two souls learning, growing, and intertwining. In this chapter, we embark on a voyage to decipher the enigma of success in relationships, a voyage that will take us through the vast landscapes of emotional connection, mutual respect, and profound partnership.

Defining success in a relationship is akin to capturing sunlight in a jar—it's radiant, elusive, and infinitely beautiful. For some, success might be synonymous with everlasting passion, an unwavering sense of belonging, or weathering the storms of life together. Others may define it through the lenses of mutual growth, the freedom to be one's true self, or the shared joys of raising a family. There is no universal blueprint for a successful relationship, for each one is as unique as the individuals who form it. However, beneath this diversity lies a common thread—a set of key elements and practices that, when woven together, form the fabric of a thriving and enduring partnership. In the chapters to come, we'll unravel these essential elements and delve into the practices that nurture love, understanding, and harmony. Join us on this exploration of the intricate tapestry of successful relationships, where the heart leads, and the mind guides.

Since one never knows how another person sees a relationship or wants from a relationship.

Here's an exercise called

Same Page: Exploring Our Vision of a Successful Relationship

Objective: To facilitate open and honest communication between partners about their shared vision of a successful relationship.

Instructions:

1. Choose a Comfortable Setting: Find a quiet and comfortable space where you can have an uninterrupted conversation.

2. Set the Mood: Light some candles, play soothing music, or create an atmosphere that promotes relaxation and intimacy.

3. Take Turns: Each partner will take turns asking and answering the following questions. Remember,

there are no right or wrong answers, and the goal is to foster understanding and connection.

 - What does a successful relationship mean to you?

 - What are the most important values and principles that should guide our relationship?

 - How do you envision our emotional connection in a successful relationship?

 - What role does trust play in our ideal relationship, and how can we nurture it?

 - In your opinion, what does effective communication look like between us?

 - How should we handle conflicts and disagreements constructively?

 - What shared goals and dreams do you believe would contribute to our relationship's success?

 - How do you see intimacy and physical affection in our ideal relationship?

 - What are some rituals or activities that you think would strengthen our bond?

4. Active Listening: As your partner responds to each question, listen attentively without

interrupting. Allow them to express their thoughts and feelings openly.

5. Share Your Own Thoughts: When it's your turn to answer, be honest and transparent about your feelings and desires for the relationship.

6. Find Common Ground: After both partners have answered all the questions, take some time to discuss areas where your visions align and where there may be differences.

7. Celebrate Similarities and Discuss Differences: Embrace the shared values and goals that you have in common and discuss how you can work together to bridge any gaps in your visions.

8. Create a Shared Vision: Based on your discussion, collaboratively create a written statement or vision for your relationship. This statement should encapsulate both partners' desires and expectations for a successful relationship.

This exercise can help couples explore their shared vision of a successful relationship, enhance communication, and align their goals and expectations. It's an opportunity to deepen your connection and strengthen your bond as you work together toward a harmonious and fulfilling partnership.

Here are three stories of couples from different backgrounds, generations, and orientations who engaged in the "Same Page: Exploring Our Vision of a Successful Relationship" exercise and discovered unexpected insights:

Sarah and Emily

Sarah and Emily, a young couple from the USA, decided to try the "Same Page" exercise to deepen their connection. They discovered that both of them highly valued spending quality time together, nurturing their emotional bond, and pursuing shared adventures. What surprised them was that Emily, who had always been more reserved about discussing the future, expressed a strong desire for long-term commitment and marriage. This unexpected revelation brought them even closer, as they realised their dreams of a lifelong partnership aligned perfectly.

Javier and Mateo

Javier and Mateo, a loving couple from Argentina in their 40s, wanted to strengthen their relationship. During the exercise, they found that their values around family, trust, and emotional support were closely aligned. However, what caught them off guard was discovering that they both had a shared dream of adopting a child, something they had never discussed before. This revelation opened up an exciting new chapter in their relationship as they began exploring the possibility of expanding their family through adoption.

Maria and David

Maria and David, a lively couple from the UK in their 60s, decided to engage in the "Same Page" exercise to rekindle their connection after many years together. As they shared their thoughts, they realised they both cherished their history together and valued their strong friendship. Unexpectedly, they discovered a mutual interest in learning to dance, which neither of them had pursued before. Embracing this shared passion, they signed up for dance lessons, igniting a newfound sense of excitement and adventure in their long-term relationship.

These stories illustrate how the exercise can lead to unexpected revelations, strengthening the bond between partners and opening doors to new shared experiences and dreams. It highlights the power of communication and alignment in fostering successful and fulfilling relationships.

Here are some key elements, sayings, wisdom, and facts on maintaining a successful partnership:

1. Communication is Key:

- Wisdom: "Communication is the foundation of a healthy relationship. It's not just about talking; it's about listening, understanding, and being present."
- Fact: Studies have shown that couples with effective communication skills are more likely to have long-lasting relationships.

2. Trust and Honesty:

- Wisdom: "Trust is built through honesty. Be transparent with each other, and trust will flourish."
- Fact: Trust issues can erode a relationship quickly, making honesty a fundamental element in successful partnerships.

3. Quality Time Together:

- Wisdom: "In the hustle and bustle of life, never forget to make time for each other. Quality time nurtures love."
- Fact: Spending quality time together strengthens emotional bonds and helps partners stay connected.

4. Respect and Equality:

- Wisdom: "Respect each other's individuality and remember that a partnership should be based on equality and mutual respect."
- Fact: Relationships built on mutual respect tend to be more satisfying and enduring.

5. Shared Values and Goals:

- Wisdom: "Partnerships thrive when you share core values and work towards common goals."
- Fact: Couples who align their values and goals are more likely to stay together and overcome challenges.

6. Patience and Forgiveness:

- Wisdom: "Patience is a virtue, and forgiveness is a choice. Both are essential for a lasting relationship."
- Fact: Couples who practice forgiveness and patience have lower stress levels and healthier relationships.

7. Emotional Intimacy:

- Wisdom: "Emotional intimacy is the secret ingredient in deepening your connection. Open your heart to each other."
- Fact: Emotional intimacy fosters a sense of security and satisfaction in relationships.

8. Compromise and Problem-Solving:

- Wisdom: "Healthy partnerships involve compromise and effective problem-solving. It's not about winning but finding solutions together."
- Fact: Successful couples learn how to navigate conflicts constructively and find mutually acceptable resolutions.

9. Laughter and Playfulness:

- Wisdom: "Laughter is the best medicine, even in relationships. Don't forget to have fun and be playful."
- Fact: Laughter reduces stress, improves mood, and enhances overall relationship satisfaction.

10. Adaptability and Growth:

- Wisdom: "Life is ever-changing, and so are you. Adapt and grow together, and your partnership will thrive."
- Fact: Couples who embrace change and personal growth together tend to have more resilient relationships.

These key elements, sayings, wisdom, and facts provide valuable insights into what makes partnerships successful. They emphasise the importance of communication, trust, respect, and emotional connection in maintaining a strong and fulfilling relationship.

Oh, and sometimes we forget… Embracing the beauty of everyday moments and real-life relationships is essential for mental wellbeing and happiness. So, I thought I would add in an extra one…

11. Embrace the Beauty of Reality:

- Wisdom: "Reality is often more beautiful than the ideals we're fed by media and society. Learn to appreciate the beauty in the ordinary moments of your relationship."
- Fact: Research has shown that couples who find joy in everyday activities and shared experiences tend to have more satisfying and enduring relationships.

This addition underscores the importance of appreciating the simple and authentic moments that real-life relationships offer, which can contribute significantly to mental wellbeing and overall happiness.

Beautifully Real

In the tapestry of life we weave,

Two souls together, we believe,

Not flawless, but perfectly real,

Embracing every scar we feel.

In flaws and quirks, our love takes flight,

For in imperfection, we find our light,

Each wrinkle, laugh line, and mistake,

A testament to love that'll never break.

The world may chase a fantasy's embrace,

But real love finds its tender place,

In everyday moments, big and small,

We celebrate the flaws that make us whole.

With mental health as our guiding star,

We heal and grow, no matter how far,

Together, we conquer storms we face,

In our love, we find a sacred space.

So let us cherish the beauty we've found,

In every up and every down,

For in our flaws, we're perfectly free,

To love, to heal, to just be "we."

CHAPTER 8

THE UNSPOKEN SYMPHONY OF EMOTIONS

In the grand theatre of love and connection, emotions play a symphony that dances between hearts. Yet, all too often, we find ourselves muting the music, concealing the rich and colourful notes of our feelings. The unspoken melodies, the hushed emotions, they too weave a tale, one that affects the tapestry of our lives. In this chapter, we embark on a journey to unearth the consequences of such emotional suppression within the intricate web of relationships. And as we traverse this uncharted terrain, we'll discover the harmonious cadence of healthy emotional expression and the transformative power of authentic communication.

The consequences of suppressing emotions in relationships and how it affects the mental health of both individuals and the couple

Suppressing emotions within a relationship is akin to burying seeds beneath the surface of the soil. Initially, it might seem like a convenient way to maintain peace and harmony. However, as time goes on, these unexpressed emotions can germinate silently, often without conscious awareness. They can manifest in various destructive ways, affecting both the individuals involved and the health of the relationship itself.

For individuals, the act of suppressing emotions can lead to heightened stress, anxiety, and even depression. It's like carrying a heavy emotional burden that constantly weighs them down. This emotional suppression can create a disconnect between their inner selves and their outward expressions, causing inner turmoil. Over time, this can erode their self-esteem and self-worth, impacting their overall mental health negatively.

Within the context of a couple, the consequences of suppressed emotions can be even more complex. Unexpressed feelings can build resentment and frustration, creating an emotional chasm between partners. It hinders authentic communication, making it challenging to resolve conflicts or deepen emotional intimacy. Ultimately, the relationship may feel strained, stifled, and unfulfilling, which can exacerbate mental health issues for both partners.

In essence, the toll of suppressing emotions in relationships cannot be underestimated. It is a silent force that gradually erodes mental well-being, both individually and as a couple. Recognising the importance of healthy emotional expression and finding effective ways to communicate these emotions can lead to a more harmonious and mentally nurturing relationship.

While we are talking about emotions, here is a list of emotions along with how they are commonly felt:

1. Happiness: Often felt as a warm, uplifting sensation in the chest. It can bring a smile to your face and a lightness in your step.

2. Sadness: Typically experienced as a heaviness in the chest or a lump in the throat. Tears may well up, and you might feel physically drained.

3. Anger: This emotion can manifest as a heat or burning sensation, particularly in the face and neck. Muscles may tense, and you might clench your fists.

4. Fear: Fear often triggers a rapid heartbeat, shallow breathing, and a sensation of butterflies in the stomach. It's a primal response designed to prepare the body to react to a perceived threat.

5. Surprise: Surprise can feel like a sudden jolt or an adrenaline rush. It might make you catch your breath or widen your eyes.

6. Disgust: Disgust can lead to a feeling of nausea or a tightening in the stomach. It might also make you physically recoil from something unpleasant.

7. Love: Love often creates a warm, expansive feeling in the chest. Your heart may feel full, and you might experience a sense of deep connection.

8. Guilt: Guilt can manifest as a heavy, sinking feeling in the gut. You may feel responsible for something negative or regretful.

9. Shame: Shame is often accompanied by a burning sensation on the face and neck. You might want to hide or withdraw from others.

10. Contentment: Contentment is a gentle, peaceful feeling. It often comes with a sense of relaxation and well-being.

11. Anxiety: Anxiety can lead to restlessness, a racing heart, and a sense of impending doom. It's often associated with worry and unease.

12. Confidence: Confidence can feel like a surge of energy and self-assuredness. Your posture may improve, and you might feel more capable.

13. Jealousy: Jealousy can create a tightness in the chest and a sense of insecurity. It often comes with thoughts of comparison to others.

14. Excitement: Excitement is characterised by a heightened state of alertness and anticipation. You might feel a burst of energy and enthusiasm.

15. Loneliness: Loneliness can bring a heavy, empty feeling in the chest. It often comes with a longing for connection.

16. Calmness: Calmness is marked by a sense of tranquillity and inner peace. Your body and mind may feel relaxed.

17. Pride: Pride can create a sense of accomplishment and self-worth. It might result in an upright posture and a feeling of satisfaction.

These descriptions provide a general sense of how emotions are commonly felt, but it's important to remember that emotional experiences can vary from person to person. Additionally, emotions are complex and often intertwined, making them unique to each individual and situation. With that in mind, and now we have an understanding of emotions – we need to delve deeper into finding a 'safe place' to express and process emotions.

Expressing and sharing emotions in a healthy way within a couple is crucial for maintaining mental health and avoiding emotional "vomiting" on each other. Here are some techniques for effective emotional expression and communication:

1. Self-Reflection: Before sharing emotions, take some time for self-reflection. Understand what you're feeling and why you're feeling that way. This can help you communicate your emotions more clearly.

2. Active Listening: When your partner is expressing their emotions, practice active listening. Pay full attention, ask clarifying questions, and validate their feelings. Avoid immediately offering solutions or advice.

3. Use "I" Statements: Instead of saying, "You always do this," use "I" statements like, "I feel hurt when this happens." This helps avoid blaming your partner and focuses on your emotions.

4. Set Boundaries: Agree on boundaries for emotional sharing. Understand when it's appropriate to discuss emotions and when it's better to wait for a calmer moment.

5. Time-Outs: If a discussion becomes too emotionally charged, agree to take a time-out. This allows both partners to cool down and return to the conversation with a clearer perspective.

6. Journaling: Encourage each other to keep a journal to privately express emotions and thoughts. Writing can be a helpful way to process feelings before sharing them.

7. Use Non-Verbal Communication: Sometimes, emotions can be expressed through non-verbal cues like body language and facial expressions. Pay attention to these signals from your partner.

8. Practice Empathy: Try to understand your partner's perspective and emotions, even if you don't agree. Empathy can help create a sense of connection and reduce emotional tension.

9. Avoid the Chain Reaction: Be mindful of how one person's emotional expression can trigger another's. Break the chain of emotional "vomiting" by practicing self-regulation and empathy.

10. Seek Professional Help: If emotional
communication within the relationship becomes
consistently challenging, consider seeking couples
therapy. A trained therapist can provide guidance
and tools for healthier communication.

Remember that healthy emotional expression and
communication take practice and patience. Both
partners should work together to create a safe and
understanding environment for sharing emotions.
This can lead to better mental health and a
stronger, more resilient relationship. It is also worth
noting that men and women experience emotions
and supress emotions in slightly different ways.
Here's a brief exploration of the differences in how
males and females may experience and express
emotions, along with subtle cues to detect
emotional suppression:

Understanding Gender Differences in Emotional Expression

While there's a wide range of individual variation, research has shown some general trends in how males and females tend to experience and express emotions:

1. Verbal Expression: Females often lean towards more verbal expression of emotions. They may talk about their feelings and seek emotional support through conversation.

2. Non-Verbal Cues: Males might rely more on non-verbal cues to express emotions. This can include body language, facial expressions, or actions rather than openly discussing feelings.

3. Social Expectations: Societal norms and gender roles can influence how emotions are expressed. Females might feel more encouraged to show vulnerability and ask for help, while males may feel societal pressure to appear strong and self-reliant.

4. Emotional Suppression: Both genders can suppress emotions, but the reasons and methods may differ. Males may suppress emotions to

conform to traditional notions of masculinity, while females might do so to maintain harmony in relationships.

Subtle Cues for Detecting Emotional Suppression

Detecting emotional suppression in a partner, regardless of gender, requires empathy, active listening, and an understanding of their unique cues. Here are some subtle signs to look for:

1. Change in Behaviour: Sudden changes in behaviour or mood can be indicative of suppressed emotions. If your partner becomes unusually withdrawn or distant, it may signal that something is amiss.

2. Physical Tension: Emotional suppression often manifests as physical tension. Look for signs like clenched fists, a rigid posture, or frequent sighs.

3. Avoidance of Topics: If your partner consistently avoids discussing certain topics or deflects conversations about emotions, they might be suppressing feelings related to those subjects.

4. Incongruence: Pay attention to incongruence between verbal and non-verbal cues. For example, if your partner says they're "fine" but their facial expressions or body language suggest otherwise, it could indicate emotional suppression.

5. Unexplained Health Issues: Chronic health problems or unexplained physical symptoms can sometimes be linked to suppressed emotions. Stress-related illnesses may surface when emotions are held back for extended periods.

6. Decreased Intimacy: Emotional suppression can impact intimacy in a relationship. If physical or emotional intimacy diminishes without an apparent reason, it's worth exploring the underlying emotional dynamics.

7. Changes in Communication Patterns: Watch for shifts in communication patterns. If your partner begins to withdraw from open and honest conversations, it could be a sign of suppressed emotions.

It's important to approach this topic with sensitivity and empathy. Encourage open and non-judgmental communication with your partner, allowing them to express their emotions in a way that feels safe and comfortable for them.

I know I keep going on about 'emotional vomit'; however, it is something I see time and time again. So, here's an insight into how emotional "vomiting" can play out in a series of interactions:

Scenario:

Sarah and Alex are in a relationship. Sarah had a tough day at work, and she's feeling frustrated and angry. She doesn't address her emotions right away and carries them with her throughout the evening. When Alex asks how her day was, she explodes with anger, accusing him of not being supportive and understanding.

Alex, taken aback by her sudden outburst, becomes defensive and responds with frustration. This triggers an argument, and both of them end up saying hurtful things they don't mean.

The next day, Sarah realises that she overreacted and emotionally "vomited" on Alex. She also notices that her outburst wasn't really about him; it was about her work-related stress.

The Chain Reaction:

Emotional "vomiting" often triggers a chain reaction. In this scenario, Sarah's anger and frustration triggered Alex's defensiveness and frustration. This, in turn, caused more anger in Sarah. The cycle continues as they both react emotionally instead of addressing the core issue.

Recognising the Pattern:

To break this pattern, it's essential to recognise when you're about to emotionally "vomit." Signs may include a sudden surge of intense emotion, physical tension, and racing thoughts. In Sarah's case, she felt a mounting sense of frustration.

Finding Healthy Outlets:

Once you recognise the signs, it's crucial to find healthy outlets for your emotions. This might involve taking a break, going for a walk, journaling, or practicing deep breathing exercises. In Sarah's case, she could have taken a few minutes to decompress and express her frustration privately before engaging in a conversation with Alex.

Effective Communication:

When you're in a calmer state, communicate your feelings and needs effectively to your partner. Sarah could have told Alex, "I had a tough day at work, and I'm feeling stressed. Can we talk about it?" This approach invites understanding and support rather than triggering defensiveness.

Seeking Solutions Together:

Finally, work together to find solutions or compromises. In Sarah and Alex's case, they could discuss ways to support each other during stressful times and create a more nurturing environment.

By recognising the pattern of emotional "vomiting," individuals can learn to manage their emotions and communicate more effectively with their partners. This can lead to healthier relationships and improved mental well-being for both parties.

It is worth recognising when you are suppressing an emotion can be a crucial step in improving emotional health and fostering healthier relationships. Emotions have a way of making themselves known, even when we try to push them down. Here are some signs that you might be suppressing an emotion:

1. Physical Tension: Suppressed emotions can manifest as physical tension in the body. You might notice muscle tightness, clenched fists, or a clenched jaw. These physical signs can be a clue that you're holding onto something.

2. Irritability: If you find yourself getting irritable or easily annoyed, it can be a sign that you're suppressing emotions. The underlying feelings may be trying to come to the surface but are being redirected as frustration.

3. Avoidance: Avoiding situations, people, or conversations that might trigger the suppressed emotion is common. If you consistently steer clear of certain topics or situations, it could indicate that you're suppressing emotions related to those issues.

4. Overreactions: Sometimes, when emotions are suppressed, they can come out unexpectedly and with greater intensity than the situation warrants. For example, you might burst into tears over a minor inconvenience because there's a backlog of unexpressed sadness or frustration.

5. Physical Symptoms: Suppressed emotions can also lead to physical symptoms such as headaches, stomach-aches, or even sleep disturbances. These physical manifestations can be your body's way of telling you that something needs to be addressed emotionally.

6. Numbing Behaviours: Engaging in numbing behaviours like excessive drinking, overeating, or binge-watching TV can be a way to avoid confronting suppressed emotions.

7. Difficulty in Relationships: Difficulty in maintaining healthy relationships can be a significant indicator. If you find it hard to connect with others, trust, or communicate openly, it could be due to unresolved emotions.

To address suppressed emotions, it's essential to practice self-awareness and self-compassion. Journaling, talking to a therapist or trusted friend, and mindfulness practices like meditation can all help you become more attuned to your emotions. Remember that it's okay to feel and express your feelings. In fact, it's a vital part of maintaining good mental and emotional health.

Well, while we are on the subject who doesn't love a good exercise/meditation? So, here's a guided mutual meditation for couples to connect with their emotions and each other:

Mutual Heart-Centred Meditation for Couples

Preparation:

1. Find a quiet, comfortable space where you won't be disturbed.

2. Sit facing each other, cross-legged, with your knees touching, about a foot apart. Your hands should rest comfortably on your own thighs.

3. Close your eyes and take a few deep breaths to centre yourselves.

Instructions:

1. Begin by synchronising your breath. Breathe in deeply and slowly through your nose for a count of four. Then exhale slowly through your mouth for a count of four. Do this together, allowing your breath to become a shared rhythm.

2. Now, gently place your right hand on your partner's heart, and your partner does the same to you. Your left hand remains on your own thigh.

3. With your hands connected to each other's hearts, continue the synchronised breathing, inhaling for a count of four and exhaling for a count of four. As you breathe, focus on the warmth and connection between your hands.

4. Begin to visualise a radiant light at the centre of your chest. This light represents your shared emotions, love, and compassion. Imagine it growing brighter with each breath.

5. Now, take a moment to think about any emotions or feelings you'd like to share or express. It could be gratitude, love, understanding, or any other emotion you'd like to communicate.

6. With each inhale, send that emotion from your heart, through your hand, and into your partner's heart. As you exhale, receive your partner's emotions in the same way.

7. Continue this process for several minutes. Feel the emotional exchange and connection between you both. If tears come, let them flow—it's a sign of emotional release and connection.

8. After some time, gradually slow your breathing and return to your normal breath. Gently release your hands from each other's hearts.

9. Take a moment to look into each other's eyes and acknowledge the emotional bond you've shared during this meditation.

10. Close the meditation with a hug or a simple "I love you."

This mutual meditation can be a powerful way for couples to deepen their emotional connection and create a safe space for sharing their feelings. It's essential to approach this practice with an open heart and without judgment, allowing each other to express emotions freely and honestly. This meditation also ties in with the 'new coming era of the heart.' Isn't that lovely!

CHAPTER 9

NAVIGATING RELATIONSHIP COMPLEXITY

Embracing the magnificence of modern love and connection, modern relationships weave a rich and diverse narrative. As we venture deeper into the 21st century, love takes on new dimensions and complexities, embracing the ever-evolving landscape of our lives. Relationships are no longer confined to traditional boundaries, but instead, they flourish amidst the beautifully complex patterns of blended families, long-distance unions, and digital connections. Yet, within these intricacies lies both the allure and the challenges of love, intricately entwined with the delicate threads of mental well-being.

In this chapter, we embark on a journey through the maze of modern relationships. We'll explore the unique dynamics of blended families, where love weaves its way through the intricate tapestry of shared histories. We'll traverse the emotional terrain of long-distance relationships, where hearts remain connected across vast distances. Amidst it all, we'll uncover the vital importance of mental well-being within the complexities of modern love. Together, we'll navigate the labyrinth of relationships, seeking wisdom, understanding, and the profound beauty that arises when we embrace the complexity of love.

Navigating Relationship Complexity and Mental Well-Being

In the elaborate landscape of modern love, we encounter the beautiful and complex tapestry of blended families. Here, love interweaves its way through shared histories, building connections that bridge the gaps between past and present. But within these blended families lie unique dynamics that can present both joys and challenges.

As the threads of love and connection merge, individuals find themselves adapting to new roles and responsibilities. Stepparents take on the nurturing of children who aren't biologically theirs, while children may need to adjust to new parental figures in their lives. It's a delicate dance where understanding, patience, and open communication become the guiding stars. Navigating these relationships can be emotionally taxing, and it's essential to acknowledge the impact on mental health.

Similarly, long-distance relationships add another layer of complexity. In a world where hearts can remain deeply connected across vast distances, couples face the challenge of maintaining intimacy and trust when physical proximity is elusive. The emotional terrain of longing and missing someone can be both heart-warming and challenging. The uncertainty of when you'll see each other again, the pangs of loneliness, and the craving for shared moments can take a toll on mental well-being.

In both blended families and long-distance relationships, the emotional rollercoaster can influence mental health and overall well-being. Feelings of stress, anxiety, or even depression may arise as individuals strive to strike a harmonious balance. Self-care, open communication, and seeking support from loved ones or professionals can be essential tools for maintaining mental well-being within these complexities of modern love. It's a journey where resilience, understanding, and the nurturing of emotional health play a pivotal role in sustaining the intricate bonds of love.

Here are some facts and examples about the changing landscape of modern relationships:

Changing Dynamics of Modern Relationships:

1. Online Dating Revolution: With the rise of technology, online dating has become the norm for many couples. In the digital age, individuals can connect with potential partners from all corners of the world, leading to diverse and multicultural relationships.

Example: A couple meets through a dating app, fostering a connection despite being from different countries. They bridge cultural gaps and celebrate their diversity, ultimately strengthening their bond.

2. Long-Distance Love: Globalisation and career opportunities often result in long-distance relationships. Couples navigate time zones and geographical distances, testing their commitment and communication skills.

Example: A married couple temporarily lives in different countries for work. They maintain their relationship through daily video calls, showing that love can thrive even when miles apart.

3. Blended Families: The concept of a traditional nuclear family has evolved. Blended families, consisting of stepparents, stepchildren, and half-siblings, create unique dynamics and emphasise the importance of effective co-parenting.

Example: After divorce, a woman marries a man with children from his previous marriage. They work diligently to create a harmonious environment for all family members, promoting understanding and acceptance.

4. Shift in Gender Roles: Modern relationships often embrace flexible gender roles, where both partners share responsibilities related to work, housekeeping, and childcare. This shift promotes equality and balance within partnerships.

Example: A couple shares household duties and childcare equally, allowing each partner to pursue their career goals while nurturing their relationship.

5. Impact of Social Media: Social media has transformed how couples interact and communicate. While it can enhance connection, it also introduces challenges related to privacy and digital boundaries.

Example: A couple faces trust issues due to one partner's excessive use of social media. They work together to set boundaries and rebuild trust, acknowledging the impact of digital communication on their relationship.

6. Delaying Marriage and Parenthood: Many couples choose to delay marriage and parenthood to focus on personal growth and career development. This trend has reshaped timelines for major life events.

Example: A couple in their 30s prioritises career stability and personal goals before deciding to get married and start a family, challenging societal norms.

These facts and examples illustrate the diverse and evolving nature of modern relationships. While they come with unique challenges, they also offer opportunities for personal growth, understanding, and lasting love. Couples today navigate a complex landscape, and their ability to adapt and communicate plays a crucial role in the success of their relationships.

Here are three fun techniques to support mental health in the changing dynamics of modern relationships:

1. "Trust Falls and Rises" Exercise (For Trust):

Trust is the foundation of any relationship, and it can be especially challenging in the digital age. To build and strengthen trust in a fun and interactive way, couples can engage in the "Trust Falls and Rises" exercise.

- How to Do It: Find a safe and open space. Stand facing each other, arms extended, and eyes closed. One partner will gently fall backward, trusting the other to catch them. After catching, they switch roles. As you do this, discuss the feeling of trust and vulnerability.
- Why It Works: This exercise combines physical trust-building with open communication about emotions. It helps partners understand the importance of trust and how it can be rebuilt when it wavers.

Trust Falls and Rises

Meet Alex and Ben, a loving couple who have been together for five years. Lately, they've been feeling a bit disconnected due to their busy work schedules and the digital distractions of modern life. They decide to try the "Trust Falls and Rises" exercise.

One sunny weekend, they head to the park, find a quiet spot, and stand facing each other with their eyes closed. Alex, the taller of the two, starts by falling backward. Ben catches him, and they laugh. Then, it's Ben's turn. As he falls backward, Alex's strong arms support him.

During the exercise, they talk about how trust is like a dance. Sometimes, you lead, and sometimes you follow, but it's always about supporting each other. They leave the park feeling more connected, their trust renewed.

2. "Family Puzzle" Activity (For Blended Families):

Blended families often face unique challenges in establishing a sense of togetherness. The "Family Puzzle" activity helps create a tangible symbol of unity.

- How to Do It: Purchase a jigsaw puzzle with enough pieces for each family member. Assemble the puzzle together, allowing each person to contribute. Discuss how each piece represents an individual and their role in the family.
- Why It Works: Completing a puzzle as a family represents the idea that every member plays a vital role in the blended family's harmony. It promotes inclusivity and a sense of belonging.

Family Puzzle

Sarah and Emily are a loving couple of ladies who recently moved in together. Both have children from previous relationships, and they want to create a sense of togetherness in their new blended family. They decide to try the "Family Puzzle" activity.

On a cosy Sunday afternoon, they gather around the dining table with their kids and open the puzzle box. Each family member chooses a piece and begins assembling it. Sarah's son, Jake, says, "I found a piece that fits with Emily's piece!" The kids are excited to contribute to the puzzle, and it quickly takes shape.

As they complete the puzzle, Sarah and Emily explain how each piece represents someone special in their family. It's a beautiful metaphor for their blended family, showing that they're all connected, even though they come from different backgrounds.

3. "Digital Detox Day" (For Social Media Communication):

In an era dominated by social media, it's essential to maintain genuine connections. The "Digital Detox Day" encourages couples to disconnect from screens for a day and focus on meaningful face-to-face interactions.

- How to Do It: Choose a day to go completely screen-free. Turn off phones, tablets, and computers. Spend quality time together engaging in activities you both enjoy, such as hiking, cooking, or playing board games.
- Why It Works: This exercise allows couples to rediscover the joy of spending uninterrupted time together. It reduces distractions, enhances communication, and fosters a deeper emotional connection

Digital Detox Day

Meet Mark and Lisa, a happy couple deeply in love, but their constant screen time is putting a strain on their relationship. They decide to have a "Digital Detox Day" to rekindle their connection.

On a sunny Saturday morning, Mark and Lisa turn off their phones and leave them in a drawer. They spend the day exploring a nearby nature reserve, enjoying a picnic, and taking photos with a regular camera.

During their hike, they rediscover the joy of uninterrupted conversation. They reminisce about their early days of dating and laugh about funny memories. Without the distraction of screens, they feel more present with each other.

At the end of the day, as they sit by a campfire roasting marshmallows, Mark says, "I love this. We should do it more often." Lisa smiles and agrees, realising that disconnecting from technology has rekindled their emotional connection.

These techniques offer enjoyable ways for couples to address trust issues, navigate the complexities of blended families, and maintain genuine communication in the digital age. They not only support mental health but also strengthen the bond between partners, making modern relationships more resilient and fulfilling. The fun also stories illustrate how couples can use unique techniques to address trust issues, navigate blended family dynamics, and improve communication in the digital age, all while promoting mental wellness and strengthening their relationships.

CHAPTER 10

SILENT BATTLES IN COUPLES

In the dance-filled dynamic of love, there are moments when the music fades, and silence takes centre stage. These are the unspoken battles that lovers often wage, hidden beneath the surface of affection and commitment. Silent battles can echo in the hearts of couples, causing ripples in the once-smooth waters of their relationship. In this chapter, we'll illuminate the shadows, exploring the whispered conflicts and unexpressed tensions that can strain even the strongest bonds. Together, we'll embark on a journey to unravel these silent battles, revealing the path to resolution and deeper connection. As we bring these hidden struggles into the light, we'll learn how to nurture the seeds of understanding, empathy, and healing in the soil of our love.

Here are some examples of silent battles in couples and a discussion of how resentment can play a role:

1. Unequal Distribution of Household Chores:

Silent Battle: One partner may feel resentful about the division of household chores. They might be doing more than their fair share but hesitate to bring it up for fear of starting an argument.

2. Financial Disagreements:

Silent Battle: Differences in spending habits or financial priorities can lead to silent battles. One partner may feel frustrated about their partner's spending choices but choose not to address it directly, leading to resentment.

3. Parenting Styles:

Silent Battle: Couples may have different approaches to parenting, leading to silent battles about discipline, screen time, or other child-rearing decisions. Resentment can build if these issues are not openly discussed and resolved.

4. Intimacy and Affection:

Silent Battle: A lack of physical intimacy or emotional affection can create silent battles in a relationship. One partner may desire more closeness but not communicate their needs, leading to resentment.

5. Unmet Expectations:

Silent Battle: When one partner has unspoken expectations about gestures of love or special occasions, such as anniversaries or birthdays, and these expectations are not met, it can lead to silent battles and resentment.

Resentment often begins with unexpressed feelings and unmet needs. When couples avoid discussing their concerns openly and honestly, these unresolved issues can fester and create a growing sense of frustration and bitterness.

Here are some facts and insights about silent battles in couples and their repercussions:

1. Impact on Mental Health: Silent battles, if left unresolved, can have a significant impact on the mental health of individuals within the relationship. The build-up of unexpressed emotions and frustration can lead to increased stress, anxiety, and even depression.

2. Communication Breakdown: Silent battles are often a result of communication breakdowns within the relationship. Failure to address issues openly can create a cycle of misunderstandings and distance between partners.

3. Relationship Satisfaction: Studies have shown that couples who engage in open and honest communication tend to report higher levels of relationship satisfaction. Conversely, couples with

unresolved silent battles are more likely to report dissatisfaction.

4. Resentment and Hostility: Over time, silent battles can escalate into resentment and hostility. What might have started as a minor disagreement or unmet need can turn into a major source of tension and conflict.

5. Physical Health Implications: Prolonged stress and negative emotions associated with silent battles can also impact physical health. It may lead to issues like sleep disturbances, headaches, and even heart problems in extreme cases.

6. Long-Term Relationship Damage: If silent battles persist for an extended period, they can erode the foundation of trust and intimacy in a relationship. This can make it challenging to rebuild and may lead to the deterioration of the partnership.

7. Parenting Impact: Silent battles can also affect parenting dynamics. Children may sense the tension and emotional distance between their parents, which can have long-lasting effects on their own emotional well-being.

8. Financial Implications: In some cases, silent battles can also extend to financial decisions. Couples may avoid discussing financial concerns, leading to financial mismanagement and debt-related stress.

It's essential for couples to recognise the signs of silent battles and actively work on improving communication and conflict resolution skills. Addressing issues openly and finding mutually satisfactory solutions can prevent the detrimental effects of unresolved conflicts in relationships.

With all of the above in mind, here are some strategies for couples to tackle these silent battles in a safe and gentle way:

1. Unequal Distribution of Household Chores:

- Open Dialogue: Initiate a calm and non-confrontational conversation about household chores. Express your feelings and concerns using "I" statements, such as "I feel overwhelmed with the workload."
- Collaborative Solution: Work together to find a chore distribution system that feels fair to both partners. Consider creating a chore chart or schedule that outlines responsibilities clearly.

- Appreciation: Acknowledge each other's efforts and express appreciation for the tasks completed. Showing gratitude can help reduce resentment.

2. Financial Disagreements:

- Regular Money Talks: Schedule regular financial discussions where you both share your financial goals and concerns. Make it a safe space to openly discuss spending habits and priorities.
- Budgeting: Create a joint budget that aligns with your shared financial goals. This can help you both track spending and make informed decisions together.
- Compromise: Recognise that financial disagreements may require compromise. Be open to finding middle ground that respects both partners' values and priorities.

3. Parenting Styles:

- Parenting Workshops: Attend parenting workshops or counseling sessions together to learn about different parenting styles and strategies. This can provide a neutral space to discuss your approaches.
- Team Approach: Frame parenting as a team effort. Emphasise the importance of working

together and finding common ground in your parenting decisions.

- Respect Differences: Acknowledge that differences in parenting styles can be beneficial. Different perspectives can provide a well-rounded approach to raising children.

4. Intimacy and Affection:

- Open Communication: Initiate a gentle conversation about your desires and needs for intimacy and affection. Share your feelings without blame or judgment.
- Quality Time: Schedule quality time together without distractions. Use this time to reconnect emotionally and physically.
- Seek Professional Help: If physical intimacy issues persist, consider seeking the guidance of a therapist or counsellor who specialises in relationships and intimacy.

5. Unmet Expectations:

- Express Expectations: Share your expectations regarding special occasions or gestures of love with your partner. Be clear about what matters to you.
- Listen Actively: Be receptive to your partner's expectations as well. Ensure you're both on the

same page about how you express love and celebrate important moments.
-   Plan Together: Collaborate on planning for special occasions to ensure they meet both partners' expectations and preferences.

In all these situations, the key is open, honest, and non-blaming communication. Both partners should feel safe expressing their feelings and concerns without fear of judgment or retaliation. Remember that finding solutions together strengthens the relationship and promotes mental well-being for both individuals.

GENDER ROLES AND RELATIONSHIP DYNAMICS

In the ever- evolving relationship terrain, an intriguing transformation is underway. The once rigid boundaries of gender roles are giving way to a more fluid, equitable, and inclusive understanding of love and partnership. As we delve into the realms of Chapter 11, we embark on a journey to explore the evolving roles of masculinity and femininity in the intricate tapestry of relationships. Here, we unravel the threads of change that lead us towards embracing neutrality and equality within partnerships.

In this chapter, we navigate the profound shifts that have taken place in our society, reshaping the way we perceive and experience love. We'll discover how understanding and embracing these changes can not only enrich our connections but also foster mental well-being, providing a loving sense of unity and togetherness. So, let us embark on this journey of exploration and transformation, where love knows no bounds and authenticity thrives.

So, with the above in mind, let's elaborate on the evolving roles of masculinity and femininity in relationships with a comparison to the past.

In the past, traditional gender roles often scripted the roles individuals played within relationships. Society had clear expectations of what it meant to be masculine or feminine, and these roles were tightly interwoven into the fabric of partnerships. Men were often the primary breadwinners, responsible for providing financial support, while women were expected to manage the household and provide emotional care. These roles, though deeply entrenched, often limited personal expression and created imbalances within relationships.

However, as we journey through time, we witness a profound transformation. Today, relationships are evolving into a more inclusive and equitable landscape, where the rigid boundaries of masculinity and femininity have softened. Men and women now share responsibilities and decision-making in ways that were once unimaginable. We see fathers taking on active parenting roles, co-parenting with mothers, and sharing household responsibilities. Women are pursuing careers, ambitions, and passions outside the home, thereby redefining the traditional feminine role.

This evolution towards embracing neutrality and equality within partnerships signifies a remarkable shift. Couples are now free to express their authentic selves without being confined by outdated stereotypes. This newfound flexibility allows individuals to explore and embody traits traditionally associated with both masculinity and femininity. Men can openly embrace vulnerability and emotional depth, while women can assert their independence and leadership with confidence. This shift not only enhances the authenticity of each partner but also enriches the dynamics of the relationship.

In the contemporary landscape of love, partnerships are becoming a harmonious blend of diverse qualities, where both partners contribute their unique strengths and energies. This shift towards neutrality and equality is not only reshaping relationships but also positively impacting mental well-being, as couples find themselves liberated from the constraints of traditional roles, forging a path towards a more loving sense of unity and togetherness.

How to Love Beyond Roles

Here's an insight into the new approach to gender roles and relationship dynamics, emphasising the evolving roles of masculinity and femininity in relationships and the importance of embracing neutrality and equality while remaining open-minded. We can refer to this approach as "How to Love Beyond Roles":

In the ever-evolving landscape of modern relationships, we find ourselves redefining the roles of masculinity and femininity. Gone are the days when these roles were rigid, prescribed by society, and bound by tradition. Today, couples have the freedom to craft their own unique dynamics, unburdened by preconceived notions.

Masculinity and femininity, once confined to specific behaviours and expectations, have transcended those boundaries. Men are encouraged to express vulnerability and sensitivity, while women explore strength and independence. The new approach to gender roles recognises that these traits are not bound by gender but are facets of human nature. It's about embracing the full spectrum of our identities, regardless of gender.

To love beyond roles means remaining open-minded, fluid, and adaptable. It means celebrating each other's individuality and the unique blend of characteristics that make your partner who they are. In lady couples, male couples, and heterosexual couples alike, this approach encourages communication, understanding, and appreciation for the beauty of the human experience in all its diversity.

As you embark on this journey of love beyond roles, remember that there are no fixed templates or rules. Each relationship is a canvas waiting for you to paint your own masterpiece. It's an opportunity to discover the depths of connection, unity, and togetherness that can be achieved when you free love from the confines of traditional roles.

Embrace the freedom to be authentically yourself and allow your partner the same privilege. Support each other's dreams and aspirations, knowing that in unity, you both shine brighter. In this new era of love, mental well-being thrives, and relationships flourish as you navigate the beautiful complexities of life together. Love beyond roles, and you'll find a love that knows no limits.

This approach to gender roles and relationships transcends labels and offers a path to deeper connection, mutual respect, and mental well-being for couples of all orientations and backgrounds. With that in mind, a poem is necessary…

How to Love Beyond Roles

In a world of expectations, where roles are defined,
Let's break the molds that limit, leave them far behind.
For love knows no boundaries, no pre-set decree,
It's a dance of hearts entwined, wild and beautifully free.

Release the shackles of convention, let them fall,
Embrace the boundless love that resides in us all.
No need for rigid roles, no need to conform,
Our love is a symphony, unique in every form.

In the warmth of your smile, I find my strength,
In your laughter, I discover immeasurable wealth.
We're partners in this journey, hand in hand we stride,
Supporting one another, in love, we both confide.

I'll be your shelter in the storm, your beacon in the night,
Together we'll conquer challenges, bask in each other's light.
In your dreams and aspirations, I'll be your biggest fan,
For in loving beyond roles, we become the best we can.

So, let's defy the norms, let love be our guide,
In this union of souls, our spirits will forever glide.
No roles can define us, no labels can confine,
In a love that knows no limits, we'll eternally shine.

With hearts wide open, in unity, we'll evolve,
In the garden of our love, our spirits will revolve.
Beyond the roles society assigns, we'll boldly soar,
For love, unbound by expectations, is worth living for.

CHAPTER 12

SOCIETAL INFLUENCES ON RELATIONSHIPS

In the spirited conga of love, couples often find themselves at the heart of a grand celebration, where the rhythm of their desires and dreams blends with the lively beats of societal expectations. The cheers, the critiques, and the ever-watchful eyes of society cast their shadows upon the love story unfolding before them. In this chapter, we'll explore the profound impact of society, culture, and external influences on couples as they navigate the unpredictable tides of their relationships. Through shared wisdom and heartfelt guidance, we'll uncover strategies to stand strong in the face of societal pressures, honouring the unique melody of love that resonates in every heart.

This chapter invites you to journey beyond the confines of societal norms, empowering you to create a relationship that shines brilliantly, guided by the authenticity of your love. Let's embark on this enlightening conga, hand in hand, as we seek to understand the forces at play and discover the strength to shape our own narrative.

Here are some insights on the impact of society, culture, and external influences on couples and how it can affect mental health and relationships:

1. Societal Expectations: Society often imposes certain expectations on couples, such as the pressure to conform to traditional gender roles or achieve specific milestones like marriage and parenthood. These expectations can create stress and lead to feelings of inadequacy or failure if not met.

2. Cultural Norms: Cultural backgrounds play a significant role in shaping relationship dynamics. Couples from diverse cultural backgrounds may face challenges related to differing values, traditions, and family expectations. Navigating these differences can be emotionally taxing.

3. External Pressures: External factors like financial stress, work-related demands, or societal prejudices can add strain to a relationship. Financial difficulties, for example, can lead to arguments and impact mental well-being.

4. Social Media and Comparison: In the age of social media, couples may find themselves comparing their relationships to idealised portrayals on platforms like Instagram. This can lead to feelings of insecurity or dissatisfaction, affecting mental health.

5. Peer Influence: Friends and family can exert influence over a couple's decisions and choices. Sometimes, well-meaning advice from loved ones can create tension or interfere with a couple's autonomy.

The impact of these societal, cultural, and external influences on mental health can be profound. Couples may experience increased stress, anxiety, or even depression as a result. It's crucial for couples to recognise these influences and find strategies to navigate them in a way that preserves their mental well-being and strengthens their relationship.

You will notice there are common themes in how to approach relationships and various challenges. They can often be applied across the board. So here are strategies for navigating societal influences on couples and promoting mental health, along with some interesting facts – that way we get to learn a few things as well as strategize!

1. Open Communication: Encourage open and honest communication with your partner about how external influences are affecting your relationship. Discuss your feelings, concerns, and expectations to ensure you both understand each other's perspectives.

Interesting Fact: Research shows that couples who communicate openly and constructively tend to have more satisfying and stable relationships.

2. Set Boundaries: Establish clear boundaries with friends and family to maintain a healthy balance between outside influences and your relationship. Politely assert your need for privacy and autonomy when necessary.

Interesting Fact: Setting boundaries in a relationship has been linked to greater relationship satisfaction and lower stress levels.

3. Cultural Exploration: Embrace and celebrate each other's cultural backgrounds. Take time to learn about and appreciate the traditions, values, and customs that are important to your partner's culture. This can foster understanding and unity.

Interesting Fact: Couples who engage in cultural exploration together often report feeling more connected and fulfilled in their relationships.

4. Digital Detox: Occasionally disconnect from social media to reduce comparison and external pressures. Designate tech-free time for meaningful interactions with your partner to strengthen your emotional connection.

Interesting Fact: Excessive social media use has been associated with higher levels of jealousy and insecurity in relationships.

5. Seek Support: If external pressures are significantly impacting your mental health or relationship, consider seeking professional support. Couples therapy or counseling can provide tools and guidance to navigate challenges effectively.

Interesting Fact: Couples therapy has been shown to be effective in improving relationship satisfaction and reducing conflict.

By implementing these strategies, couples can better navigate societal influences, protect their mental well-being, and build a resilient and fulfilling relationship. Remember that every relationship is unique, and it's essential to find what works best for you and your partner.

Here are three stories illustrating the impact of societal influences on couples from different backgrounds:

Nurturing Love Beyond Borders

Emma and Maria, a lady couple in their 30s from different cultural backgrounds, faced societal expectations about marriage. Emma's conservative family believed in traditional marriages, while Maria's family embraced more progressive values. This caused tension and emotional distress for the couple.

They decided to have an open conversation about their feelings and concerns. Through dialogue, they found common ground and set boundaries with their families. They chose to focus on their love rather than societal pressures. This strengthened their bond and improved their mental well-being.

Breaking Free from Stereotypes

Mark and James, a male couple in their 40s, felt the weight of societal stereotypes about masculinity. Mark struggled with expressing vulnerability, fearing it would challenge his masculinity. James encouraged him to embrace his emotions, leading to a more authentic connection.

They attended couples therapy, where they learned strategies to challenge stereotypes and support each other's emotional well-being. By rejecting societal norms and embracing their true selves, they cultivated a more fulfilling relationship.

Unplugging for Love

Sarah and David, a young couple in their 20s, experienced the negative effects of social media comparison. Constantly comparing their relationship to others online, they felt inadequate. It began to affect their mental health and created distance between them.

Recognising the issue, they decided to implement a digital detox. They set aside time for meaningful face-to-face conversations, limiting social media use. This allowed them to rekindle their connection and prioritise their mental well-being.

In each story, the couples faced unique challenges stemming from societal expectations, cultural norms, or social media pressures. However, by addressing these issues head-on and finding solutions that worked for them, they not only preserved their relationships but also improved their mental health and well-being.

CHAPTER 13

VULNERABILITY AND AUTHENTICITY

In the vagaries of vulnerability, we discover the true essence of love. It's within the tender moments of sharing our fears, hopes, and imperfections that the most profound connections are forged. This chapter explores the pivotal role of vulnerability in weaving trust and intimacy, inviting us to embrace authenticity and openness in our relationships.

The Importance of Vulnerability in Building Trust and Intimacy:

Vulnerability is the fertile soil in which trust and intimacy take root and flourish. It's the act of willingly exposing our true selves, with all our strengths and vulnerabilities, to our partners. When we allow ourselves to be vulnerable, we send a powerful message that we trust our loved ones enough to show them our unguarded hearts. This, in turn, encourages reciprocity, creating a safe space where both partners can share their deepest feelings and thoughts without fear of judgment.

Vulnerability is the bridge that connects us on a profound emotional level. It allows us to access the hidden chambers of our hearts, where our most authentic desires and fears reside. By being open and honest about our emotions, we invite our partners to do the same, fostering a deep sense of connection. It's through vulnerability that we can truly understand and support one another, and it's the cornerstone of building lasting trust and intimacy in relationships.

Encouraging Authenticity and Openness in Relationships:

Authenticity and openness are the twin pillars upon which healthy, thriving relationships stand. Authenticity involves being true to oneself and one's feelings, while openness is about transparently sharing those feelings with our partner. These qualities create an environment of mutual respect and understanding.

Encouraging authenticity means embracing both our strengths and our weaknesses. It means acknowledging our own imperfections and accepting our partners without judgment. It's about celebrating the unique qualities that make us who we are. When we encourage authenticity in our relationships, we promote a sense of safety where our partners can be their true selves.

Openness is the willingness to communicate openly and honestly. It's sharing our thoughts, feelings, desires, and concerns with our partner. Openness fosters emotional intimacy and ensures that both partners are on the same page. By promoting openness, we create an environment where issues can be discussed and resolved, rather than left to fester and potentially harm the relationship.

Together, authenticity and openness create an atmosphere in which both partners can feel seen, heard, and valued. They allow love to flourish in its purest form, where individuals can grow and evolve together while maintaining their unique identities.

Okay, so being vulnerable is challenging, well it is for me. There are times I have felt physically sick when having to be vulnerable. So, with that as a powerful driver, here's an explanation of how to allow oneself to be vulnerable and why vulnerability is powerful:

Easiest Ways to Allow Oneself to Be Vulnerable:

1. Share Your Feelings: Start by sharing your feelings, even the ones that might make you feel exposed. This could be as simple as expressing when you're feeling sad, happy, anxious, or overwhelmed.

2. Admit Mistakes: Acknowledge when you've made a mistake or when you're unsure about something. Admitting imperfection is a powerful form of vulnerability.

3. Ask for Help: Don't hesitate to ask for support or help from your partner when you need it. This can be about emotional support, assistance with tasks, or advice.

4. Express Desires and Needs: Share your desires, needs, and boundaries with your partner. This includes discussing what you want from the relationship, both emotionally and physically.

5. Share Your Past: Open up about your past experiences, including your fears, insecurities, and past traumas. Sharing your history can foster understanding and empathy.

6. Be Honest About Your Vulnerabilities: If you're feeling particularly vulnerable or anxious, let your partner know. Sometimes, just sharing that you're struggling can be a powerful act of vulnerability.

Why Vulnerability Is Powerful:

Vulnerability is a powerful force in relationships because it builds trust, deepens emotional connection, and fosters authenticity. When you're vulnerable with your partner, you're essentially saying, "I trust you with my deepest self." This trust is the foundation upon which love and intimacy are built.

Vulnerability allows you to connect on a profound level. When you share your true self, warts and all, you create a space for your partner to do the same. This exchange of vulnerability can lead to a deeper understanding of each other's needs, desires, and fears.

In terms of mental health, vulnerability is liberating. It enables you to release pent-up emotions and confront issues head-on. Instead of bottling up feelings or anxieties, you're addressing them in a healthy way. This can alleviate stress and reduce the risk of developing mental health issues like anxiety or depression.

Moreover, vulnerability can inspire others to be vulnerable too. When you open up to your partner, you create a safe and accepting environment. This can encourage them to reciprocate, allowing both of you to experience the profound benefits of emotional intimacy. In turn, this mutual vulnerability can strengthen your relationship and lead to improved mental well-being for both partners.

The power of vulnerability lies in its ability to nurture deep connections, promote emotional healing, and encourage personal growth within the context of a loving relationship.

Once we have allowed ourselves to be vulnerable then why not encourage authenticity and openness too?

Encouraging Authenticity:

Authenticity is about being true to yourself and expressing your thoughts, feelings, and desires honestly. In a world where many people wear masks and create facades, encouraging authenticity in relationships is like giving the gift of genuine connection. To be authentic, one must first understand themselves. Self-awareness is key. Reflect on your values, beliefs, and what truly matters to you. Accept your flaws and imperfections; they make you unique. Embrace vulnerability and share your true self with your partner. Authenticity also means setting healthy boundaries. Don't pretend to be someone you're not or suppress your emotions to please others. When you're authentic, you invite your partner to do the same, creating a deeper and more meaningful connection.

The Power of Openness:

Openness is the gateway to trust, understanding, and emotional intimacy. It involves sharing not only the positive aspects of your life but also your fears, insecurities, and challenges. Openness allows you to connect on a profound level. It's a powerful tool for conflict resolution because it promotes empathy and compassion. When you're open with your partner, you invite them into your inner world, fostering a sense of togetherness. Openness inspires growth and personal development. It encourages both partners to learn and evolve together. In a relationship where openness thrives, you can weather life's storms with greater resilience. Being open also sets an example for your partner, encouraging them to be more open as well. It's a chain reaction that leads to a stronger, healthier connection.

Promoting authenticity and openness in relationships not only deepens the bond between partners but also contributes to better mental health. It provides a safe space for emotional expression, reducing stress and anxiety. When both individuals can be themselves without fear of judgment, it creates an environment where they can support and uplift each other. Authenticity and openness inspire trust and empathy, making it easier to navigate the challenges that arise in any relationship.

Here are three stories that illustrate the power of vulnerability, authenticity, and openness in relationships:

Breaking the Armor - A Journey of Vulnerability

Meet Maria and Elena, a loving couple from diverse cultural backgrounds. Over the years, Maria had built a protective armor around herself, afraid to show vulnerability. One day, she decided to share her deepest fears and insecurities with Elena. As she shed her protective layers, Elena embraced her with love and understanding. This newfound vulnerability strengthened their bond, creating a space for trust and emotional connection. In the process, Maria also discovered that opening up improved her mental health. She found relief in expressing her emotions and realised that vulnerability was a powerful tool for healing.

Unveiling the Authentic Self

Meet Sarah and James, a married couple with decades between them. Sarah had always been the composed, responsible one, but she had hidden a passionate artist deep within her. She decided to share her artistic side with James. As he encouraged her to embrace her true self, she felt an overwhelming sense of liberation. This act of authenticity not only deepened their connection but also transformed Sarah's mental well-being. She had suppressed her artistic passion for years, and now, she felt a profound sense of completeness, which had a positive impact on her overall mental health.

The Power of Openness

Meet Mark and David, a loving couple from different cultural backgrounds. They had always been open with each other, discussing their joys and struggles openly. This openness allowed them to navigate life's challenges together, including Mark's struggle with anxiety. Mark's willingness to share his feelings with David made it easier for him to seek professional help. David's unwavering support was a pillar of strength during this journey. Through openness and support, Mark's mental health improved significantly. Their relationship was a testament to the power of transparency and its positive impact on mental well-being.

In each of these stories, the couples discovered the transformative power of vulnerability, authenticity, and openness. These revelations not only strengthened their relationships but also had a profound effect on their mental health, helping them find hidden depths within themselves and embrace a more authentic and fulfilling life.

CHAPTER 14

NAVIGATING ANXIETY AND DEPRESSION HAND IN HAND

Within the delicate duality of emotions, relationships often find themselves facing a formidable duo: anxiety and depression. These formidable states of mind are not exclusive to any individual, and when they knock on the door of love, the response can shape the path ahead. In the pages of this chapter, we embark on a journey to understand how to be each other's anchor when the waves of anxiety and the shadows of depression loom. We'll explore ways to nurture not only our partner's mental well-being but also the collective strength of the relationship itself. So, let us delve into the realm of emotions, arm in arm, ready to navigate these challenging waters together.

Here are some facts and insights about anxiety and depression in couples, along with an elaboration on their impact on mental health and relationships:

Anxiety and Depression in Couples: Facts and Insights

1. Prevalence: Anxiety disorders and depression are prevalent in many societies worldwide. It's estimated that around 1 in 3 people will experience an anxiety disorder or depression at some point in their lives.

2. Impact on Relationships: These mental health conditions can significantly affect relationships. Individuals with anxiety or depression may struggle with emotional regulation, communication, and intimacy, which can strain the partnership.

3. Communication Challenges: Anxiety can lead to excessive worry, while depression often involves feelings of sadness, hopelessness, and fatigue. These emotions can make it challenging for couples to communicate openly and effectively.

4. Emotional Withdrawal: Depression can sometimes lead to emotional withdrawal or numbness, causing one partner to feel distant and disconnected from the other. This emotional distance can create tension in the relationship.

5. Support and Understanding: Couples who navigate anxiety and depression together often build a deeper level of understanding, empathy, and support. This shared experience can strengthen their bond.

6. Seeking Professional Help: It's crucial for couples facing anxiety and depression to seek professional help when needed. Therapy and counseling can provide valuable tools for managing these conditions individually and as a couple.

The Impact on Mental Health and Relationships

Anxiety and depression can have a profound impact on mental health and relationships:

- Emotional Strain: These conditions can lead to emotional strain within the relationship. The affected individual may experience intense emotions, making it challenging to maintain a sense of balance and harmony.

- Communication Hurdles: Anxiety and depression can disrupt effective communication. Individuals may find it difficult to express their needs and emotions, which can lead to misunderstandings and conflicts.

- Isolation: Both conditions can contribute to feelings of isolation. An individual with anxiety or depression may isolate themselves from their partner, leading to a sense of loneliness within the relationship.

- Support and Resilience: On the positive side, navigating anxiety and depression together can foster resilience. Couples who work through these challenges may develop a stronger, more supportive partnership.

- Professional Help: Seeking professional help is crucial for managing anxiety and depression. Couples therapy or counseling can provide tools to cope with these conditions and strengthen the relationship.

Supporting a partner dealing with anxiety or depression while maintaining mental well-being as a couple can provide challenges. Although when approached with empathy, resilience, and love such challenges can be transformed and increase closeness within the relationship. Since we are human, we will always discover that our humanness can enable connection.

Here are some cues to notice anxiety and depression in a partner and tips on how to broach the subject with kindness:

Cues to Notice Anxiety and Depression in a Partner:

1. Changes in Mood: Pay attention to significant and prolonged changes in your partner's mood. If they seem consistently sad, irritable, or anxious, it could be a sign.

2. Loss of Interest: Notice if your partner loses interest in activities they once enjoyed. Depression often leads to a lack of motivation and interest in hobbies or socialising.

3. Appetite and Sleep Changes: Significant changes in eating or sleeping patterns, such as increased or decreased appetite, insomnia, or oversleeping, can be indicators.

4. Physical Symptoms: Keep an eye out for physical symptoms like headaches, digestive issues, or unexplained aches and pains, which can be associated with anxiety and depression.

5. Energy Levels: A decrease in energy and persistent fatigue may point to depression, while heightened anxiety can result in restlessness and hyperactivity.

6. Withdrawal: If your partner becomes socially withdrawn, avoids gatherings, or isolates themselves, it might be a sign of emotional distress.

7. Negative Self-Talk: Listen for self-critical or negative self-talk. People with anxiety or depression may express feelings of worthlessness or hopelessness.

Broaching the Subject with Kindness:

1. Choose the Right Time and Place: Find a quiet and comfortable environment where you both feel safe to talk openly. Avoid discussing sensitive topics during arguments or in public.

2. Use "I" Statements: Start the conversation with "I" statements to express your feelings and concerns without placing blame. For example, say, "I've noticed some changes in your mood lately, and I'm concerned."

3. Express Empathy: Show empathy and understanding. Let your partner know that you're there to support them, and you care about their well-being.

4. Ask Open-Ended Questions: Encourage open dialogue by asking open-ended questions like, "How have you been feeling lately?" This invites your partner to share without feeling pressured.

5. Avoid Judgment: Refrain from making judgments or offering quick solutions. Instead, actively listen and validate their feelings.

6. Offer Support: Let your partner know that you're willing to support them in seeking help, whether it's through therapy, counselling, or medical professionals.

7. Respect Their Pace: Understand that your partner may need time to process and accept what they're going through. Respect their pace in seeking help or sharing more about their feelings.

8. Avoid Pressure: Don't pressure your partner into discussing their emotions if they're not ready. Offer your support but respect their boundaries.

9. Stay Calm and Patient: Stay calm and patient throughout the conversation. Keep in mind that discussing mental health can be challenging, and emotions may run high.

10. Seek Professional Help: If your partner acknowledges their struggles with anxiety or depression, encourage them to seek professional help. Offer to assist in finding a therapist or counsellor.

Approaching the subject of anxiety and depression with kindness, empathy, and understanding can create a safe space for your partner to share their feelings and seek the help they may need. It's essential to prioritise their well-being and offer support throughout their journey to mental health and healing.

Withdrawn With Loss of Interest

Meet Sarah and Emily, a loving couple living in California. They've been together for six years. Lately, Sarah has noticed changes in Emily's behaviour. She's become withdrawn, lost interest in their shared hobbies, and often cries without apparent reason. Recognising these signs, Sarah sits down with Emily in the cosy living room of their San Francisco apartment. With empathy and concern, she gently says, "Emily, I've noticed that you've been feeling down lately. I'm here for you, and I want to support you in any way I can." Emily, feeling understood and cared for, opens up about her struggles with anxiety. Together, they explore therapy options, and their journey towards healing strengthens their bond.

Strong and Silent…

In a small town in the UK, Kate and James have been married for 20 years. In the 1980s, mental health discussions were less common. James has always been the strong, silent type and struggles with depression. He hides his feelings, not wanting to burden Kate. One day, Kate stumbles upon a book about depression and its impact on relationships. She realises that James might be suffering in silence. With great care, she broaches the subject. "James, I love you, and I've noticed you seem distant lately. We're a team, and I want to understand what you're going through." This conversation leads James to open up about his feelings, and together, they seek counseling, helping them navigate James' depression and fostering a deeper connection.

Pillar of Strength

Carlos and Miguel, a gorgeous couple from Brazil, have been together for a decade. They come from different cultural backgrounds but share a strong bond. One evening, Miguel, who has always been the pillar of strength in their relationship, reveals that he's been battling anxiety for years. Carlos listens attentively, realising that Miguel's stoic exterior has concealed his emotional turmoil. They hold each other, tears in their eyes, as Carlos says, "Miguel, you don't have to face this alone. We're a team, and I'm here to support you." Miguel's vulnerability becomes a turning point, as they seek therapy together and learn how to navigate Miguel's anxiety as a couple.

These stories illustrate how couples from diverse backgrounds and eras can face mental health challenges with love and support, emphasising the importance of open communication, empathy, and seeking help when needed.

I realised that I would be interested in knowing what the common causes of anxiety and depression are, that way I could understand my partner and be more empathetic. So, here's a list of common causes and triggers of anxiety and depression:

Common Causes of Anxiety:

1. Stress: High levels of stress from work, relationships, or life events can trigger anxiety.
2. Trauma: Past traumatic experiences, such as abuse or accidents, can lead to anxiety disorders.
3. Genetics: A family history of anxiety can increase the risk of developing an anxiety disorder.
4. Personality: Certain personality traits, like perfectionism or a tendency to worry, may make individuals more prone to anxiety.
5. Medical Conditions: Chronic illnesses, hormonal imbalances, and certain medications can contribute to anxiety.
6. Substance Abuse: Drug or alcohol abuse can exacerbate or trigger anxiety disorders.
7. Neurochemical Imbalance: An imbalance in brain chemicals (neurotransmitters) can contribute to anxiety.
8. Chronic Illness: Dealing with a long-term illness can lead to health-related anxiety.

9. Major Life Changes: Events like divorce, job loss, or moving to a new location can cause anxiety.
10. Phobias: Specific phobias, such as fear of flying or heights, can lead to anxiety when confronted with triggers.

Common Causes of Depression:

1. Genetics: A family history of depression can increase the risk of developing depression.
2. Brain Chemistry: An imbalance of neurotransmitters, such as serotonin, can play a role in depression.
3. Life Events: Major life changes, loss of a loved one, or trauma can trigger depression.
4. Chronic Illness: Managing a long-term illness can lead to depression.
5. Substance Abuse: Drug or alcohol abuse can contribute to depressive disorders.
6. Personality: Certain personality traits, like a pessimistic outlook or low self-esteem, can make individuals more susceptible.
7. Hormonal Changes: Hormonal fluctuations during pregnancy, postpartum, or menopause can lead to depression.
8. Social Isolation: Lack of social support or loneliness can contribute to depressive feelings.

9. Work or School Stress: High levels of stress in professional or academic life can lead to depression.
10. Other Mental Health Conditions: Conditions like anxiety, bipolar disorder, or eating disorders can co-occur with depression.

It's important to remember that these causes can interact and vary from person to person. Seek professional help if you or someone you know is experiencing symptoms of anxiety or depression.

Here are some approaches and wisdom for couples dealing with anxiety and depression:

Approaches for Couples Dealing with Anxiety and Depression:

1. Open and Compassionate Communication: Foster an environment where both partners feel safe to express their thoughts and feelings. Encourage open dialogue without judgment or pressure to "fix" the issue. Listening with empathy can provide immense relief for the person with anxiety or depression.

2. Seek Professional Help: Understand that anxiety and depression are medical conditions that may require professional treatment. Encourage your partner to seek therapy, counselling, or medication as recommended by a mental health professional. Supporting their journey toward healing is an act of love.

3. Educate Yourself: Learn about anxiety and depression to gain insight into what your partner is experiencing. Understanding the conditions can reduce misunderstandings and misconceptions, fostering empathy and connection.

4. Create a Routine: Structure and routine can provide a sense of stability for both partners. Establishing healthy daily habits, including exercise, a balanced diet, and quality sleep, can contribute to improved mental well-being.

5. Practice Patience: Healing takes time, and there may be setbacks along the way. Be patient with your partner and yourself and avoid placing unrealistic expectations on the pace of recovery.

Wisdom for Couples:

- Love is a Healing Force: Love has the power to uplift, support, and heal. Approach your partner's journey with love as your guiding light. Let your love be a source of strength during challenging times.

- In Unity, there is Strength: Remember that you are a team, facing life's challenges together. Lean on each other for support and draw strength from your partnership. Together, you can overcome even the most daunting obstacles.

- Embrace Imperfection: Both you and your partner are imperfect beings, and that's perfectly okay. Accept the imperfections and vulnerabilities in each other, for it is in those moments of vulnerability that true connection and growth can occur.

- Self-Care is Not Selfish: Taking care of your own mental health is not selfish; it's essential. Ensure that you maintain your well-being so that you can continue to be a pillar of support for your partner.

- Seek Joy Amidst Challenges: Even in the midst of anxiety and depression, moments of joy, laughter, and connection can be found. Cherish these moments and celebrate them together. They are the beacons of hope on the path to healing.

Remember that navigating anxiety and depression as a couple is a journey that requires patience, understanding, and unwavering support. By approaching it together with love and resilience, you can emerge from the darkness into the light of healing and growth.

CHAPTER 15

BODY IMAGE AND SELF-ESTEEM IN RELATIONSHIPS

In the intricate choreography of relationships, where hearts and souls entwine, the mirrors we hold to ourselves often reflect the perceptions of our beloved. Our bodies, these sacred vessels, carry the stories of our journeys, etched in every curve and line. Yet, within the embrace of love, these temples sometimes become battlegrounds for insecurities, triggering ripples of doubt and discord in the dance of partnership. In this chapter, we step into the profound arena of body image and self-esteem within relationships, where perceptions of beauty and self-worth intertwine with the threads of love and acceptance. We'll explore how body image issues can cast shadows on the stage of love and delve into the empowering strategies that illuminate the path to self-acceptance, a healthy body image, and the radiant mental well-being that blossoms from within. For, in the realm of love, the most captivating beauty lies in the authenticity of our souls and the boundless, loving acceptance we offer ourselves and our partners.

Body image issues can affect couples in many ways and these issues may differ between males and females. Here are some interesting facts:

How Body Image Issues Can Affect Couples:

In the dance of love, body image issues can cast long shadows, affecting couples in profound ways. These issues may lead to feelings of insecurity, inadequacy, and self-doubt, which can impact the dynamics of the relationship. For individuals with body image concerns, intimacy may be hindered by a fear of vulnerability. They may avoid physical contact, struggle with self-confidence, or develop negative self-talk. Additionally, these insecurities can lead to decreased satisfaction in the relationship, as one's own perceived flaws may overshadow the positive aspects of the partnership.

Gender Differences in Body Image Issues:

Body image issues can manifest differently between males and females, often influenced by societal norms and expectations. In many cultures, females are exposed to ideals of slimness and flawless beauty, which can lead to body dissatisfaction and disordered eating. On the other hand, males may experience pressure to conform to muscular or athletic ideals, potentially triggering body dysmorphia or excessive exercise. It's important to recognise that both genders can struggle with body image, and open dialogue within the relationship can foster empathy and support.

Interesting Facts:

- Research shows that media exposure to idealised body images can lead to negative body image perceptions in both men and women.
- Men are increasingly reporting body dissatisfaction, with a rise in concerns about muscle size and tone.
- Negative body image can lead to higher levels of stress, anxiety, and depression, impacting not only mental health but also the quality of relationships.

Understanding these nuances of body image and its influence on couples is essential for cultivating empathy, fostering open communication, and promoting self-acceptance within relationships.

Males and females may internalise body image issues and can impact their mental states:

Internalisation of Body Image Issues:

Both males and females can internalise body image issues, but they may do so in unique ways due to societal pressures and gender norms.

- Females: Women often internalise the pressure to conform to unrealistic beauty standards. They may criticise themselves for not meeting these standards, leading to negative self-talk and reduced self-esteem. This internalisation can manifest as feelings of inadequacy, shame, and self-doubt. Women may engage in behaviours like excessive dieting or cosmetic procedures to try to attain the perceived ideal body, which can further exacerbate mental health challenges.

- Males: Men, too, face the pressure of body ideals, often linked to muscularity and athleticism. They may internalise these ideals by obsessing over their physique, spending excessive time in the gym, or even resorting to steroids or other performance-enhancing substances. This can lead to a condition known as muscle dysmorphia, where men constantly feel small and physically inadequate. Such internalisation can result in heightened anxiety, depression, and self-esteem issues.

Impact on Mental States:

Internalising body image issues can significantly impact the mental states of both males and females:

- Anxiety and Depression: Feelings of inadequacy and the constant pursuit of an idealised body can lead to anxiety and depression in both genders. These mental health challenges can affect the overall well-being of individuals and, by extension, their relationships.
- Low Self-Esteem: Internalised body image issues often erode self-esteem. Both males and females may struggle with feelings of self-worth, leading to diminished confidence and difficulty in expressing vulnerability within their relationships.
- Relationship Strain: When individuals internalise body image issues, it can strain their relationships. Insecurities may lead to avoidance of physical intimacy, difficulty in accepting compliments, or even jealousy. These dynamics can create tension and hinder emotional connection.

Understanding how males and females internalise body image issues is essential for couples to provide each other with empathy and support. Open and non-judgmental communication can help individuals address these issues together and work toward promoting self-acceptance and a healthier body image.

Here are two exercises to help individuals and couples cultivate love and appreciation for their bodies:

Cultivating Self-Love for Your Body and Cells (Individual)

1. Find a quiet and comfortable space where you can sit or lie down without distractions.

2. Close your eyes and take several deep, slow breaths to centre yourself.

3. Begin to focus your attention on your body. Visualise your body at the cellular level, with trillions of cells working tirelessly to keep you alive and well.

4. In your mind, silently repeat the following affirmations or similar positive statements:

-   "I love and appreciate my body."
-   "My cells work together for my well-being."
-   "I am grateful for my body's resilience."

- "I am worthy of love and care, including self-love."

5. As you repeat these affirmations, imagine a warm, golden light surrounding your body and infusing each cell with love and gratitude.

6. Continue this practice for at least 10-15 minutes, allowing yourself to feel a growing sense of love and appreciation for your body and its incredible abilities.

Mutual Body Appreciation (Couples)

1. Find a quiet and comfortable space where you can sit cross-legged, facing each other.

2. Hold hands or place your hands on each other's hearts.

3. Close your eyes and take a few deep breaths together to create a sense of connection.

4. One person begins by expressing something they appreciate about their partner's body. This can be a specific feature, a quality, or something more general. For example, "I appreciate your strong arms; they make me feel safe."

5. After sharing, the partner receiving the compliment responds with gratitude and reciprocates with their own appreciation. For

example, "Thank you; I love your warm smile. It brightens my day."

6. Continue taking turns, moving around the body or focusing on different aspects of each other's physical selves. Be specific and sincere in your compliments.

7. As you share appreciations, allow yourselves to really connect with each other's bodies through touch and affection.

8. Take your time with this exercise, allowing it to unfold naturally. It's an opportunity to express love and gratitude for each other's bodies and the unique qualities that make you feel drawn to one another.

These exercises can foster a deeper sense of self-love and body acceptance for individuals and enhance the connection and appreciation between partners in a relationship.

Here are three stories of couples from different backgrounds who participated in the self-love and body appreciation exercises and the positive impact it had on their mental health and self-esteem:

Anna and Sophie - The Netherlands

Anna and Sophie, a loving couple from The Netherlands, decided to try the self-love and body appreciation exercises together. As they sat facing each other, holding hands and exchanging compliments, they felt a deeper connection forming. Anna shared how she appreciated Sophie's strong and graceful posture, while Sophie admired Anna's beautiful, expressive eyes.

Over time, these exercises became a regular practice in their relationship. They found that by openly expressing their admiration for each other's bodies, their self-esteem and confidence grew. This newfound self-pride reflected in other aspects of their lives, helping them face challenges with resilience. Their mental health improved as they learned to embrace and cherish themselves and each other, finding strength in vulnerability.

Carlos and Javier - Costa Rica

Carlos and Javier, a male couple from Costa Rica, embarked on the self-love and body appreciation journey together. In the beginning, they felt somewhat hesitant to openly express their admiration for each other's bodies. However, as they continued the practice, they discovered a deeper level of intimacy and connection.

Carlos appreciated Javier's strong and nurturing embrace, while Javier admired Carlos's sense of humour and infectious laughter. These exercises helped them break down barriers they had built around their self-esteem. They realised that loving and accepting themselves was the foundation for loving and accepting each other fully.

As their self-pride grew, Carlos and Javier felt more secure in their relationship. They faced the world as a united front, armed with newfound self-confidence and a strengthened mental well-being.

Sarah and Mark - New Zealand

Sarah and Mark, a cheeky couple from New Zealand, decided to try the mutual body appreciation exercise. Sitting cross-legged, they began expressing their gratitude for each other's bodies. Sarah complimented Mark's strong, capable hands, while Mark appreciated Sarah's beautiful, radiant smile.

These exercises became a cherished ritual for Sarah and Mark. They found that openly appreciating each other's bodies helped them overcome insecurities they had carried for years. The positivity radiated from their physical connection to their emotional bond, making them feel more secure in themselves and their relationship.

As their self-esteem improved, Sarah and Mark felt more resilient in dealing with life's challenges. They also noticed a significant positive shift in their mental health. They realised that embracing their bodies and openly expressing their admiration for each other had a profound impact on their overall well-being.

These stories demonstrate how self-love and body appreciation exercises can positively impact individuals and couples from various backgrounds, enhancing self-esteem, strengthening relationships, and promoting mental well-being.

Cultivating body love both individually and in relationships can have a profound positive impact on one's mental health. Here's an additional insight:

Cultivating Body Love for Mental Well-Being:

Embracing and celebrating your own body, as well as appreciating your partner's, can lead to improved mental health and overall well-being. When individuals practice self-love and body acceptance, it fosters a sense of self-pride and self-worth. This, in turn, contributes to positive mental states, including reduced anxiety and depression.

For individuals, developing body love involves acknowledging and accepting their bodies as they are, celebrating their uniqueness, and reframing negative self-talk. This self-compassion can alleviate the mental burden of unrealistic beauty standards and the stress of feeling inadequate.

In relationships, openly expressing admiration for each other's bodies creates a safe and loving space where both partners feel valued and accepted. It deepens emotional intimacy and strengthens the emotional connection. This mutual appreciation promotes a sense of security and belonging, reducing feelings of loneliness or isolation that can negatively impact mental health.

As individuals and couples nurture body love, they become more resilient to external pressures and judgments. They are better equipped to face life's challenges with a positive mindset, knowing that they are loved and accepted for who they are, both inside and out.

By incorporating these practices into their daily lives, individuals and couples can experience improved mental health, increased self-confidence, and a greater capacity for love and compassion towards themselves and each other. Body love becomes a powerful tool for promoting mental well-being and fostering more fulfilling and harmonious relationships. While we are feeling inspired…

TO LOVE OUR BODIES

In the mirror's gentle gaze, we find our grace,
Embracing every line and curve in this sacred space.
For this vessel, a masterpiece, our body, our own,
A temple of beauty and strength, brightly shown.

In the warmth of your eyes, I see my reflection,
A love so deep, it defies all imperfection.
We celebrate every scar, every freckle, every trace,
In your embrace, I find my safe place.

Together we stand, hand in hand, heart to heart,
No judgment, no shame, just love from the start.
With each whispered "I love you," our spirits take
flight,
In this dance of pure love, we find endless light.

Our bodies, our allies, our partners in grace,
Together, we cherish, in this loving embrace.
For body love blooms in the garden we sow,
With every touch, every kiss, love continues to
grow.

So, let us honour this gift, this love we have found,
In our bodies' sweet symphony, forever unbound.
With self-love as our guide, we journey as one,
In the embrace of body love, our hearts become
one.

May this poem inspire you to cherish and celebrate
your own body and your partner's body with love
and acceptance, nurturing a bond of deep
connection and self-pride.

CHAPTER 16

BALANCING WORK AND LOVE

In the rhythmic routine of modern life, we often find ourselves juggling multiple roles and responsibilities. We step into the bustling world of work, striving for success, growth, and fulfilment. Simultaneously, we cherish the intimate bonds of love, yearning for connection, understanding, and affection. Balancing these intricate threads, weaving the fabric of a fulfilling career with the tapestry of a loving relationship, is a delicate artistry.

As we navigate the demands of our careers and the desires of our hearts, we discover the profound importance of equilibrium—the harmony that allows us to excel professionally without neglecting the sanctuary of love. In this chapter, we delve into the realm of work and love, exploring strategies to harmonise these essential dimensions of life. We'll unravel the complexities of managing career demands while nurturing a thriving relationship, ultimately achieving a healthy work-life-love balance. In this exploration, we uncover the secrets to maintaining mental well-being, fostering happiness, and igniting the fires of love amidst the bustling world of work.

In today's fast-paced world, many of us dedicate a significant portion of our day to work-related activities. When you consider the hours spent commuting, the time at the workplace, and sometimes the additional hours of bringing work-related concerns home, it can seem like work dominates our lives. On average, many individuals spend around 8-10 hours per day at work, which equates to nearly half of the waking hours in a typical day.

In contrast, the time we allocate to our relationships, including our partners, family, and friends, often takes up a smaller portion of our day. Factors like work demands, long commutes, and technological distractions can sometimes limit the quality time we invest in our relationships. It's not uncommon for people to feel the strain of balancing career aspirations with maintaining meaningful connections.

Understanding this imbalance is crucial for achieving a healthy work-life-love balance. While it's important to excel in our careers, it's equally important to nurture our relationships, as they provide the emotional support, companionship, and love that enrich our lives. Striking the right balance between work and love can significantly impact our overall well-being and happiness.

Here are ten interesting facts about work-life balance, mental health, and relationships:

1. Balanced Work-Life Improves Mental Health: Studies show that individuals who maintain a healthy work-life balance experience lower levels of stress, reduced risk of burnout, and improved mental health.

2. Time Spent at Work: On average, people spend a significant portion of their adult lives at work, approximately 90,000 hours or about one-third of their total waking hours.

3. Impact on Relationships: A poor work-life balance can strain relationships. Couples who find it challenging to balance work and personal life may experience increased conflict and dissatisfaction.

4. Technology's Influence: The increasing use of technology and remote work can blur the lines between work and personal life, making it harder to maintain a healthy balance.

5. Vacation Time: Surprisingly, many employees don't use all their allotted vacation days. This can lead to increased stress and decreased mental well-being.

6. Mental Health Days: Some companies are recognising the importance of mental health by offering "mental health days" as part of their employee benefits, acknowledging the need to take time off for emotional well-being.

7. Dual-Career Couples: In dual-career couples, balancing work and personal life can be particularly challenging. These couples often face complex scheduling issues and may struggle to find quality time together.

8. Flexible Work Arrangements: Flexible work arrangements, such as remote work or flexible hours, can help improve work-life balance and reduce stress for employees.

9. Impact on Children: A parent's work-life balance significantly affects their children's well-being. Spending quality time with children is crucial for their emotional development.

10. Financial Stress: Financial stress resulting from work-related issues or job loss can have a severe impact on relationships and mental health. Couples often need to navigate financial challenges together.

These facts highlight the intricate relationship between work, mental health, and relationships, emphasising the importance of finding a healthy balance to nurture both personal well-being and meaningful connections with loved ones.

Finding time for both a fulfilling relationship and self-care can be an ongoing challenge. Here are some key points to consider:

1. Time Management: Balancing work, personal life, and a relationship requires effective time management. It's essential to prioritise both your partner and yourself by setting boundaries around work hours and allocating quality time for your relationship. This might involve creating a shared calendar, where you schedule date nights or quality time together.

2. Self-Care Rituals: Self-care is crucial for maintaining your mental and emotional well-being. These rituals can include exercise, meditation, hobbies, or simply spending time alone to recharge. Prioritising self-care not only benefits you but also strengthens your relationship by allowing you to show up as your best self.

3. Communication: Open and honest communication with your partner is vital. Discuss your individual needs for personal time and self-care. This helps you both understand each other's priorities and can lead to finding mutually beneficial solutions.

4. Quality Over Quantity: While finding long stretches of time for your relationship and self-care may be challenging, remember that quality often trumps quantity. Even short, meaningful interactions with your partner and focused self-care moments can have a significant impact.

5. Delegate and Share Responsibilities: Don't hesitate to delegate or share responsibilities, both in your relationship and personal life. This can include dividing household chores, involving family or friends for support, or seeking help with childcare if applicable.

6. Boundaries: Setting clear boundaries between work, relationship, and self-care time is essential. Boundaries help prevent burnout and ensure that you can fully engage in each aspect of your life without feeling overwhelmed.

7. Flexibility: Be flexible and adaptable. Life can be unpredictable, and sometimes work or personal obligations may demand more time than expected. Understanding and flexibility within your relationship can help you navigate these challenges together.

Remember that finding the right balance between your relationship and self-care is an ongoing process. It requires awareness, communication, and a commitment to nurturing both aspects of your life for optimal mental well-being and happiness.

Here are three examples of couples achieving work-life balance:

Quality and Flexibility

Sarah and Emma, a married couple in their mid-30s, both had demanding careers in marketing and finance. They struggled to spend quality time together and noticed the toll it was taking on their relationship. To achieve better work-life balance, they took the following steps:

1. Communication: They openly discussed their career goals and personal priorities. They realised that they both valued their relationship and decided to make it a priority.

2. Flexible Schedules: Sarah negotiated a flexible work arrangement that allowed her to work from home two days a week. Emma adjusted her hours to have a shorter workday, giving them more time together.

3. Shared Responsibilities: They divided household chores and responsibilities evenly to reduce stress. This allowed them to have more quality time together.

Careers and Children

Javier and Diego, a glorious couple in their early 40s, had adopted two children. Balancing their careers and parenting duties was challenging. Here's how they achieved work-life balance:

1. Parenting Support: They established a strong support network of friends and family who could help with childcare when needed. This gave them opportunities for date nights and self-care.

2. Synced Schedules: They synchronised their work schedules to minimise the time their children spent in day-care. They coordinated their vacations and flexible hours to be there for their kids.

3. Quality Family Time: They made a conscious effort to create quality family time. Weekends were dedicated to family activities like hiking and picnics, fostering a strong bond with their children.

Busy and Need Balance

Emily and Mark, a busy couple in their late 20s, were both ambitious professionals. They faced the challenge of maintaining work-life balance early in their careers. Here's what they did:

1. Prioritising Time Together: They scheduled "no-work" evenings where they would put away their devices and focus on each other. This helped strengthen their emotional connection.

2. Time Management: Emily and Mark became more efficient at work, enabling them to leave the office on time. This allowed them to have dinner together regularly and engage in shared hobbies.

3. Shared Responsibilities: They divided household chores and responsibilities evenly, reducing the burden of domestic work and freeing up more time for leisure activities.

These real-life examples demonstrate that achieving work-life balance is possible with open communication, flexible schedules, and a commitment to prioritising one's relationship and personal well-being.

Work-Life-Love Balance

A few other things to bear in mind to enable a work-life-love balance:

- Flexibility and Adaptability: Remind readers that achieving balance may require adjustments over time. Be flexible and willing to adapt to changing circumstances and priorities.

- Support Networks: Encourage individuals and couples to build a strong support network of friends and family who can provide assistance and understanding during busy or challenging periods.

- Regular Check-Ins: Suggest the practice of regular check-ins with one's partner to discuss work-life-love balance. Open and honest communication can help address any issues or concerns.

- Goal Setting: Encourage setting both individual and relationship goals. Having shared aspirations can motivate couples to work together to achieve balance.

- Celebrating Small Wins: Remind people to celebrate their achievements, no matter how small. Recognising progress can boost motivation and reinforce the importance of maintaining balance.

- Role Models: Share stories of individuals or couples who have successfully achieved work-life-love balance. Hearing about real-life examples can be inspiring.

- Continuous Learning: Stress that achieving balance is an ongoing journey. Encourage a commitment to continuous learning and adaptation as life evolves.

By highlighting these aspects, you can inspire individuals and couples to prioritise their relationships and overall well-being while navigating the challenges of modern life and work demands.

CHAPTER 17

PERSEVERANCE AND GROWTH

In the joyous journey of love, marked by its joys and tribulations, one quality stands tall as a guiding star – perseverance. Relationships, like life itself, are a journey of growth, marked by moments of triumph and adversity. It's during the challenging times that perseverance becomes the gentle yet resolute hand that guides us through the darkness toward the light of growth and transformation.

In this chapter, we explore the vital role of perseverance in overcoming the inevitable challenges that arise in every relationship. We'll delve into the wisdom of those who have weathered storms together, emerging stronger and wiser. Alongside perseverance, we'll unveil strategies for continuous personal and relational growth, painting a portrait of love's enduring strength and the boundless potential for renewal that awaits those who embrace its journey."

Here's an insight into how couples who have been together for over fifty years have achieved enduring perseverance in spite of adversities:

In the loopiness of love, there are stories that stand as timeless testaments to the power of perseverance. Couples who have celebrated over fifty years of togetherness are living embodiments of unwavering commitment. Their journey has weathered the storms of life, and they've emerged stronger, hand in hand. What is it that keeps these couples together through thick and thin?

One key insight lies in their ability to adapt and evolve. These couples have not clung to the past but have grown together, continuously reinventing their relationship as they navigate life's twists and turns. They have faced trials – financial struggles, health challenges, family dynamics – with an unyielding belief in their love's resilience.

Moreover, communication and empathy play pivotal roles. Long-lasting couples have honed their skills in understanding each other's needs, even in the most trying moments. They've learned that disagreements can be opportunities for growth, and forgiveness is the glue that mends the inevitable fractures.

Ultimately, these couples have a shared sense of purpose – a commitment to building a life together that is greater than the sum of its parts. Their perseverance isn't merely a matter of enduring; it's a relentless pursuit of happiness and a deep-rooted faith in the transformative power of love. Their stories serve as guiding stars for those embarking on the journey of enduring love, reminding us of all that, with the right partner and unwavering perseverance, love can truly conquer all."

Once upon a time, high in the picturesque Austrian Alps, there lived a couple whose love story was as enduring as the majestic mountains that surrounded them. Friedrich, at the ripe age of 99, and Gertrude, his 97-year-old beloved, had spent nearly eight decades together, weathering life's storms with unwavering love.

Their love story began when they were just teenagers, growing up in the same quaint village nestled amidst the lush green meadows and towering peaks. From the moment they met, there was a spark between them that no one could deny. They courted under the shade of blossoming apple trees and danced together at the village's summer festivals. They knew they were meant to be.

As the years passed, they faced their share of challenges. World War II brought separation and uncertainty, as Friedrich was drafted into the military. Gertrude waited faithfully, writing letters of love and longing. When the war finally ended, they were reunited, their love stronger than ever.

Through all the ups and downs, Friedrich and Gertrude discovered five secrets to their enduring love:

1. Communication: They talked openly about their hopes, dreams, and fears. They never let misunderstandings fester, and they resolved conflicts by listening to each other with empathy.

2. Forgiveness: Forgiving each other for mistakes, large and small, was crucial. They understood that holding onto grudges would only create distance between them.

3. Shared Dreams: They had shared goals and dreams for their future. Whether it was building their cosy mountain cabin or traveling to distant lands, they always had something to look forward to together.

4. Quality Time: Friedrich and Gertrude made sure to spend quality time with each other. They took long walks in the meadows, picnicked by crystal-clear streams, and stargazed on clear, moonlit nights.

5. Unconditional Support: They were each other's greatest cheerleaders. In times of illness or hardship, they leaned on one another for unwavering support and comfort.

As they sat by the fireplace in their cosy cabin, Friedrich and Gertrude reflected on their remarkable journey together. They knew they were incredibly fortunate to have found a love so enduring. Their love had not only weathered the

test of time but had also brought warmth and light
to everyone they met.

Their story was a testament to the power of love,
communication, and forgiveness. They were living
proof that love could conquer all challenges, and
they hoped their story would inspire others to
cherish and nurture their own love, no matter the
obstacles life might present.

The Secret of Love: Insights Through the Ages

Love, the timeless force that binds hearts and souls together, has been a subject of fascination and exploration for centuries. From ancient philosophers to modern-day romantics, the pursuit of the secret to enduring love has been a shared quest. Through the ages, five key secrets have emerged to help us maintain and cherish the profound connections we find in our lives:

1. Communication: Plato, the Greek philosopher, wisely noted that "At the touch of love, everyone becomes a poet." Love inspires us to find the right words and expressions to convey our feelings. The secret lies in open, honest, and empathetic communication. Share your thoughts, dreams, and fears with your loved one. Listen actively and understand their perspective. The more you communicate, the deeper your connection will grow.

2. Compassion: As the Dalai Lama teaches, "Love and compassion are necessities, not luxuries. Without them, humanity cannot survive." Compassion forms the foundation of love. It means being kind, forgiving, and understanding towards your partner. In moments of vulnerability and weakness, a compassionate heart can mend even the deepest wounds.

3. Shared Experiences: Antoine de Saint-Exupéry, the author of "The Little Prince," reminded us that "Love does not consist in gazing at each other but in looking outward together in the same direction." Love is a journey, and shared experiences enrich that journey. Travel, explore, and create memories together. These shared moments become the threads of your unique tapestry of love.

4. Resilience: Winston Churchill, who navigated through some of the darkest times in history, shared a valuable insight: "Success is not final, failure is not fatal: It is the courage to continue that counts." Relationships face challenges, but the secret lies in resilience. When love faces adversity, it is the determination to weather the storms together that makes it stronger.

5. Unconditional Acceptance: Maya Angelou, the renowned poet, declared, "Love recognises no barriers. It jumps hurdles, leaps fences, penetrates walls to arrive at its destination full of hope." The greatest secret of love is accepting your partner unconditionally. Embrace their flaws and quirks, for they make them unique. Love them not in spite of their imperfections but because of them.

These five timeless secrets have transcended generations, cultures, and continents. They remind us that love is not a destination but a continuous journey. By nurturing these qualities in our hearts and relationships, we unlock the secret of love's enduring power. Love is not about perfection; it's about connection, understanding, and the willingness to keep growing, side by side, through the ages.

CHAPTER 18

EMPOWERMENT AND HAPPINESS IN RELATIONSHIPS

In the resonant radiance of love, empowerment and happiness weave intricate patterns of connection and fulfilment. Relationships, like gardens, require constant nurturing to flourish. As we embark on this chapter, we'll explore the vital role empowerment and happiness play in crafting a love story that stands the test of time.

Our journey begins with the understanding that empowerment is not just an individual pursuit but a collective endeavour. It is the art of finding strength within oneself to uplift not only our lives but also the life we share with our partner. Empowerment fuels our sense of self-worth, fuels our ambitions, and enables us to become the best versions of ourselves within a relationship.

Happiness, the radiant sun of emotional well-being, bathes our connections in warmth and light. When we are happy, we naturally radiate positivity and kindness, creating an environment where love can thrive. It is both a destination and a path, an ever-evolving state of being that transforms our relationships into a haven of joy and contentment.

In the chapters to come, we will unravel the threads of empowerment and happiness. We'll explore the individual and collective journey of self-discovery, growth, and fulfilment. Through wisdom, inspiration, and practical strategies, we will illuminate the path to a relationship where empowerment and happiness are not just sought after but are embraced as a way of life. Together, we will craft a blueprint for a love story that is rich in both strength and joy, where every page reveals the beauty of empowerment and happiness in the tapestry of love.

Talking of empowerment, it is worth understanding co-dependency in contrast to co-independence.

Mental Well-being and Co-dependence in Relationships:

Mental well-being plays a crucial role in the dynamics of healthy relationships. When individuals within a partnership prioritise their own mental health, it sets the foundation for a more balanced and fulfilling connection. However, co-dependent dynamics can sometimes emerge and affect mental well-being within a relationship.

Co-dependence is a relational pattern where one person becomes excessively reliant on the other for emotional support, validation, and a sense of identity. It often involves enabling unhealthy behaviours, such as addiction or enabling excessive self-sacrifice to meet the needs of the other person.

Here are some key points:

1. Balancing Independence and Interdependence: Healthy relationships strike a balance between independence (maintaining one's individuality and self-care) and interdependence (mutual reliance and support). Both partners should feel secure in themselves while also supporting each other.

2. Maintaining Boundaries: Setting and respecting boundaries is essential for mental well-being. It ensures that each person's needs and autonomy are honoured. Boundaries help prevent co-dependent tendencies from taking root.

3. Communication and Self-Awareness: Open and honest communication is vital. Partners should feel comfortable discussing their mental health, needs, and concerns without fear of judgment. Self-awareness and emotional intelligence play a role in

recognising co-dependent patterns and addressing them.

4. Seeking Professional Help: In cases where co-dependency or mental health issues are significant, seeking professional guidance, such as therapy or counselling, can be immensely beneficial. These experts can provide tools and strategies for healthier relationship dynamics and improved mental well-being.

5. Supporting Growth: Healthy relationships encourage personal growth and development. Partners should inspire each other to pursue their passions, hobbies, and self-care routines that contribute to mental well-being.

By fostering an environment of mutual respect, open communication, and self-awareness, couples can navigate the complexities of mental well-being and co-dependency in a way that strengthens their bond and individual happiness.

Co-independence is a term used to describe a balanced and healthy form of interdependence in a relationship. Unlike co-dependence, where one partner relies excessively on the other, co-independence emphasises mutual support, respect, and shared growth while still maintaining individuality. Here's how co-independence works:

1. Mutual Support: In co-independent relationships, both partners actively support each other's goals, dreams, and well-being. They encourage each other to pursue their passions and interests while offering emotional and practical support.

2. Respect for Individuality: Co-independence acknowledges and respects each partner's individuality. It allows for differences in opinions, interests, and boundaries without judgment. Partners recognise that they are two unique individuals with their own needs and desires.

3. Healthy Boundaries: Co-independent couples establish and respect healthy boundaries. This means that both individuals can express their needs and feelings without fear of criticism or control. Boundaries are clear and communicated openly.

4. Communication: Open and honest communication is a cornerstone of co-independence. Partners feel comfortable discussing their thoughts, feelings, and concerns with each other. They actively listen and validate each other's experiences.

5. Shared Growth: Co-independent relationships foster an environment where personal growth and mutual growth are equally valued. Partners inspire each other to learn, evolve, and become the best versions of themselves.

6. Emotional Interdependence: While respecting individuality, co-independent couples share emotional interdependence. They rely on each other for emotional support, understanding, and love, but they do so without losing their own sense of self.

7. Conflict Resolution: In co-independent relationships, conflicts are approached as opportunities for growth and understanding. Partners work together to find solutions and resolve disagreements in a respectful and constructive manner.

8. Self-Care: Co-independent couples prioritise self-care and encourage each other to engage in activities that promote mental and emotional well-being. They understand that taking care of themselves individually contributes to a healthier relationship.

9. Mutual Goals: Co-independent partners often have shared goals and values. They collaborate on building a life together that aligns with their shared vision while respecting each other's aspirations.

Co-independence promotes a harmonious and loving partnership where both individuals feel secure, valued, and empowered. It acknowledges that a strong relationship is built on the foundation of two fulfilled individuals who come together to create something even more beautiful.

As mentioned before there are common tools within relationships. In this case similar tools have been applied to Empowerment and Happiness. However, what we realise is each tool can be adapted accordingly.

Here are some of the best and easiest ways to approach these essential elements and contribute to relationship success:

1. Self-Discovery and Personal Growth:

- Take time for introspection to understand your own needs, desires, and values.
- Set personal goals and work towards them, both individually and as a couple.
- Encourage your partner's personal growth by supporting their aspirations.

2. Effective Communication:

- Practice active listening, which involves truly hearing and understanding your partner's perspective.
- Express your thoughts, feelings, and needs openly and honestly, fostering a safe space for open dialogue.
- Learn to resolve conflicts constructively, focusing on solutions rather than blame.

3. Shared Goals and Dreams:

- Identify common interests and aspirations, and set shared goals as a couple.
- Celebrate achievements together, no matter how small, to reinforce the sense of partnership.
- Revisit and adapt your goals over time as your relationship evolves.

4. Emotional Intimacy:

- Cultivate emotional intimacy by sharing your vulnerabilities and fears with your partner.
- Offer and receive emotional support, creating a sense of safety and trust.
- Engage in activities that promote emotional connection, such as deep conversations or shared hobbies.

5. Gratitude and Positivity:

- Practice gratitude by regularly acknowledging and appreciating each other's contributions.
- Focus on positive aspects of your relationship and celebrate the moments of joy.
- Avoid dwelling on negativity and work together to find solutions to challenges.

6. Self-Care and Well-Being:

- Prioritise self-care to maintain your mental and physical health, which directly impacts your happiness.
- Encourage your partner to engage in self-care activities that bring them joy and relaxation.
- Understand that taking care of yourself allows you to be a better partner.

7. Support and Encouragement:

- Offer unwavering support and encouragement to your partner's pursuits and dreams.
- Be a source of motivation and inspiration, cheering each other on during life's ups and downs.
- Celebrate each other's achievements as a team.

8. Balance and Boundaries:

- Maintain a healthy balance between your personal life, work, and relationship.
- Set clear boundaries to protect your time and energy, ensuring that you both have space to recharge.
- Respect each other's boundaries and individual needs.

9. Quality Time and Connection:

- Dedicate quality time to connect, away from distractions, screens, and daily stressors.
- Create rituals or traditions that deepen your connection, such as date nights or shared hobbies.
- Remember the importance of physical touch, hugs, and affection in nurturing your bond.

10. Continuous Learning:

- Stay open to learning and growing together, adapting to changes and challenges.
- Explore new experiences, take on challenges, and learn from your shared adventures.
- Keep an attitude of curiosity and exploration, fostering a sense of vitality and freshness in your relationship.

By incorporating these approaches into your relationship, you can embark on a shared journey of empowerment and happiness, building a strong foundation for lasting success and fulfilment together.

While we are on the subject, here are two empowering and fun exercises designed to enhance love, happiness, and empowerment in your relationship:

Empowering Love - "Affirmation Exchange"

In this exercise, you and your partner will exchange empowering affirmations to boost each other's self-esteem and reinforce your love. Find a comfortable and quiet space to sit facing each other.

1. Preparation:

- Each of you should take a few moments to reflect on the qualities you admire in your partner. Think about their strengths, positive characteristics, and the impact they've had on your life.

2. Affirmation Exchange:

- One at a time, take turns expressing affirmations to your partner. Begin each affirmation with "I admire..." or "I appreciate..." and be specific about what you value in them.

- For example, you might say, "I admire your unwavering support and kindness. You make me a better person."
- Allow your partner to receive the affirmation with gratitude and an open heart.

3. Reflect and Respond:

- After each affirmation, take a moment to reflect on how it made you feel to hear those words from your partner.
- Respond with a heartfelt thank you or share any emotions that arise.

4. Switch Roles:

- Once you've both had a chance to exchange affirmations, switch roles, and allow your partner to affirm you.
- Continue until you both feel uplifted and deeply appreciated.

Loving, Happiness, and Us - "Dream Collage"

This creative and playful exercise allows you to envision your shared happiness and future together. It's a wonderful way to bond over your dreams and aspirations.

1. Gather Supplies:

- Collect magazines, scissors, glue, a large sheet of paper or poster board, and markers or coloured pencils.

2. Create Your Dream Collage:

- Sit down together with the supplies and the intention to create a "Dream Collage" for your relationship.
- Each of you should flip through the magazines and cut out images, words, or phrases that represent your individual dreams and goals.
- Glue these elements onto the large sheet of paper or poster board, arranging them in a collage.

3. Share and Discuss:

- Once the collage is complete, take turns
  sharing what each element represents and
  how it relates to your dreams and happiness.
- Discuss how your individual dreams can align
  with your shared goals as a couple.

4. Collaborate on the Future:

- Identify common dreams and aspirations that
  you both share.
- Use markers or coloured pencils to draw
  connecting lines between elements that
  symbolise your shared goals.
- Discuss how you can support each other in
  achieving these dreams and creating
  happiness together.

5. Display Your Dream Collage:

- Find a special place to display your Dream
  Collage in your home as a reminder of your
  shared vision for the future.

These exercises not only strengthen your bond but
also empower each of you to celebrate your
uniqueness and cultivate happiness in your

relationship. Enjoy the process of growth, love, and shared dreams!

Here are three heart-warming stories of couples from different backgrounds and regions who undertook the "Empowering Love" and "Dream Collage" exercises:

Edda and Elín from Iceland

Edda and Elín, a loving couple from Iceland, decided to try the exercises one cosy winter evening. As they exchanged affirmations in the "Empowering Love" exercise, Edda's eyes welled up with tears when Elín expressed how much she admired Edda's unwavering strength and resilience. Edda, in return, told Elín how her kindness and empathy brought warmth to her life.

Inspired by their affirmations, they delved into the "Dream Collage" exercise. Amid the serene landscapes of Iceland, they cut out images of snowy mountains, cosy homes, and vibrant wildflowers, signifying their shared dreams of building a peaceful life together. As they glued these elements onto the poster board, they realised how aligned their aspirations truly were. This exercise strengthened their commitment to supporting each other's goals while nurturing their shared dreams of a harmonious future.

Raj and Priya from Singapore

Raj and Priya, a chirpy couple from Singapore, embarked on the exercises one sunny afternoon. During the "Empowering Love" exchange, Priya spoke from her heart about how Raj's dedication to their family and his unwavering support empowered her every day. Raj, in turn, praised Priya's resilience and her ability to find joy in life's simplest moments.

With enthusiasm, they dived into the "Dream Collage" exercise, cutting out images of exotic destinations, a cosy home with a white picket fence, and family gatherings. They pasted these images onto their poster board, representing their dreams of adventure and togetherness. As they discussed each element, they realised that their shared dreams of exploring the world and creating lasting memories were entirely attainable. This exercise rekindled their sense of adventure and deepened their appreciation for one another.

Liam and Ethan from Australia

Liam and Ethan, a devoted male couple from Australia, chose a warm, sunny day for the exercises. During the "Empowering Love" exercise, Ethan's heartfelt words about Liam's creativity and resilience touched Liam deeply. Liam, in return, celebrated Ethan's unwavering commitment and emotional intelligence.

They then embraced the "Dream Collage" exercise, cutting out images of beaches, art studios, and thriving gardens, symbolising their shared dreams of a beachside home filled with creativity and love. As they created their collage, they realised how their dreams of a peaceful, artistic life intertwined. Their shared vision and commitment to living life to the fullest deepened their bond, igniting a renewed sense of purpose and happiness.

In each of these unique love stories, the exercises allowed couples to celebrate their love, affirm each other's strengths, and align their dreams. They discovered that empowerment and happiness, when nurtured individually and together, led to even stronger and more fulfilling relationships. Whether in Iceland, Singapore, or Australia, the exercises became a universal path to love, growth, and happiness in these couples' lives.

CHAPTER 19

NAVIGATING THE NEW RELATIONSHIP LANDSCAPE

In the adapting and evolving randomness of human existence, relationships have woven a story as intricate as it is beautiful. As we journey through life's diverse landscapes, we find ourselves amidst a changing world, one that constantly shapes the dynamics of our connections with one another. This chapter explores the art of navigating the new relationship landscape, where the threads of love, commitment, and partnership intertwine with the forces of technology, societal shifts, and the ever-expanding horizon of human potential.

In the past, relationships were often confined to certain norms and expectations, but today, we stand at the threshold of a new era, one filled with opportunities for deeper connections and unprecedented possibilities. With open hearts and open minds, we delve into the transformative power of love in a world that continues to evolve. Together, let us prepare for the future of relationships, where compassion, understanding, and resilience will be our guiding stars through this uncharted territory.

The speed of change in our modern world is unprecedented, and it profoundly affects relationships and mental health. Here's an exploration of these aspects:

The Speed of Change:

In the digital age, change occurs at an accelerated pace. Technological advancements, shifts in societal norms, and changes in work structures have reshaped how we live and interact. This rapid transformation can create both opportunities and challenges for relationships.

Anticipated Changes:

Anticipating the changes on the horizon is crucial for relationship adaptability. Some of the anticipated changes include:

1. Technology Integration: Continued integration of technology into our lives, from virtual reality to artificial intelligence, will change how we communicate and connect.

2. Work-Life Integration: The lines between work and personal life will continue to blur, impacting how couples manage time and prioritise each other.

3. Social Shifts: Evolving societal norms, such as changing gender roles and acceptance of diverse relationship structures, will influence how couples define their relationships.

4. Mental Health Awareness: Increasing awareness and acceptance of mental health issues will play a significant role in how couples address and support each other's well-being.

Impact on Relationships and Mental Health:

- Communication: Constant connectivity can lead to information overload and reduced quality time together. Couples must prioritise meaningful communication amidst the digital noise.

- Work-Life Balance: The pressure to be always available for work can strain relationships. Couples must establish boundaries and prioritise self-care.

- Social Comparisons: Social media can lead to unhealthy comparisons, affecting self-esteem and mental health. Couples should promote authenticity and focus on shared values.

- Mental Health Stigma: While mental health awareness is growing, stigma can still affect individuals and couples. Open conversations and seeking professional help when needed are essential.

Adaptation and Evolution:

To adapt and thrive in this changing landscape, couples can:

1. Prioritise Connection: Make intentional efforts to connect emotionally, even in a fast-paced world. Set aside time for meaningful conversations and shared activities.

2. Flexible Roles: Embrace flexible and evolving roles within the relationship. Support each other's personal growth and changing aspirations.

3. Tech Boundaries: Set healthy boundaries with technology. Designate tech-free times and spaces to foster in-person connection.

4. Mental Health Support: Normalise discussions about mental health and seek professional help when necessary. Understand that supporting each other's well-being is a fundamental aspect of a healthy relationship.

5. Lifelong Learning: Commit to lifelong learning and personal growth. Encourage each other to adapt to new challenges and opportunities.

In the face of rapid change, relationships can remain resilient and nurturing by valuing connection, flexibility, and mutual support. By adapting and evolving together, couples can navigate the new relationship landscape while maintaining their mental well-being and deepening their love.

Here are stories and wisdom from various couples on how they coped with the speed of change and anticipated changes in technology integration, work-life balance, social shifts, and mental health awareness:

The Resilient Couple - Embracing Technology:

Sarah and Emma, a couple from Sweden, found themselves navigating the fast-paced changes in technology. Instead of resisting it, they embraced the benefits. They integrated virtual reality into their date nights, exploring new worlds together. Their wisdom: "Change can be an opportunity for shared growth. Embrace it together."

The Adaptable Couple - Redefining Gender Roles:

Juan and Carlos, a couple from Mexico, faced shifting gender norms and work-life integration challenges. They learned to balance their careers while taking turns managing household responsibilities. Their wisdom: "Flexibility in roles strengthens our bond and allows us to support each other's dreams."

The Diverse Couple - Celebrating Differences:

Sophie and David, a cheeky couple from South Africa, navigated evolving societal norms and mental health awareness. They realised that each partner's unique qualities were strengths that enriched their relationship. Their wisdom: "Our differences are our greatest assets. Together, we're unstoppable."

The Compassionate Couple - Prioritising Mental Health:

Lisa and Mark, another interesting couple from Canada, prioritised mental health awareness. They openly discussed their emotional well-being and encouraged each other to seek professional help when needed. Their wisdom: "Love means being there for each other in good times and bad, especially when it comes to mental health."

The Tech-Savvy Couple - Tech Boundaries:

Maria and Sofia, a couple from Brazil, understood the importance of setting tech boundaries. They designated "unplugged" evenings and focused on connecting without digital distractions. Their wisdom: "Disconnect to reconnect. Our relationship thrives in those offline moments."

The Work-Life Balancing Couple - Creating Space:

Kai and Hiroshi, a couple from Japan, grappled with work-life integration challenges. They created a designated "work-free zone" at home where they could unwind and connect. Their wisdom: "Creating space for love amid the hustle and bustle keeps us grounded."

These stories and wisdom reflect the diversity and resilience of couples in adapting to changes. They emphasise the importance of embracing change, supporting each other, and finding new ways to connect and grow together in the face of anticipated changes in our evolving world.

Embracing the Bright Future of Love

In a world that is constantly changing, relationships stand at the forefront of change, adaptation, and boundless possibilities. The future of love is not a daunting abyss but a horizon that promises new adventures, deeper connections, and limitless opportunities for growth.

Understanding Ourselves:

To embark on this journey, we must first understand ourselves. Our mental health, our dreams, and our desires are the compasses that guide us through the complexities of modern relationships. The mirror we hold to our souls reflects not only our own growth but also our capacity to inspire others.

Mental Health as a Foundation:

Mental health is the bedrock upon which strong, resilient relationships are built. The future beckons us to prioritise emotional well-being, to communicate openly about our struggles, and to offer unwavering support to our partners. Together, we navigate the labyrinth of emotions, emerging stronger and more connected than ever before.

The Speed of Change as an Ally:

Change is not our adversary; it is our ally. The speed at which our world transforms invites us to innovate, to adapt, and to stay curious. It pushes us to find new ways to kindle the flames of romance, to cherish each moment, and to celebrate the quirks that make our relationships uniquely beautiful.

Embrace, Love, Inspire:

The future is a canvas awaiting our strokes of love, acceptance, and inspiration. As we embrace the unknown, we embark on a journey of self-discovery and shared growth. Each day is an opportunity to kindle the fires of passion, to laugh together, and to dance to the rhythm of our own hearts.

Bright Horizons Await:

In this new era of love, we stand at the threshold of infinite possibilities. The future is bright, and our love is the beacon that guides us through uncharted waters. Let us step forward hand in hand, embracing the brilliance of what's to come, and savouring the joy of love, connection, and shared adventures.

The future of relationships is not a destination; it is an ongoing, vibrant journey. Together, we paint the tapestry of love with the vivid colours of understanding, compassion, and empowerment. As we look ahead, let us do so with hope, excitement, and the knowledge that the best is yet to come.

CHAPTER 20

CONCLUSION: NAVIGATING THE JOURNEY TOWARDS LOVE, WELLNESS, AND WHOLENESS

As we reach the culmination of our exploration into the elaborate play of love, wellness, and wholeness, we find ourselves at the crossroads of understanding, growth, and boundless possibilities. Throughout this transformative journey, we have delved deep into the recesses of our hearts and minds, seeking wisdom, insight, and the keys to nurturing relationships that heal, empower, and flourish.

Lessons Learned:

Our voyage has illuminated the significance of mental wellness, revealing that the well-being of individuals is the cornerstone upon which the foundation of a thriving relationship is built. We have learned that by tending to our own emotional landscapes, we become better equipped to traverse the shared terrain of love and connection. We've discovered that vulnerability is not a sign of weakness but a wellspring of strength, forging bonds that transcend the boundaries of time and circumstance.

Mental Wellness—Individually and as a Couple:

The journey has affirmed that mental wellness is not a solitary pursuit but a shared endeavour. It thrives in the embrace of empathy, compassion, and open communication. Together, we have explored the intricate dance of attachment styles, delved into the profound neuroscience of love, and harnessed the power of mirror neurons to deepen our emotional connections.

Moving Forward into a New Dawn:

As we stand on the threshold of a new dawn, we do so with hope, excitement, and an unwavering commitment to love, empower, and heal. We carry with us the insights of those who have weathered the storms of time and emerged with hearts aglow with enduring affection. We are armed with strategies to confront the challenges of modern life and societal pressures, recognising that change is not our foe but our collaborator in shaping a brighter future.

Review and Share with Others:

This journey has been both personal and collective, as we have woven our stories into the rich tapestry of human experience. To fully embrace the wisdom we have uncovered, we invite you to review and reflect upon these insights. Share them with others, extending the gift of knowledge, compassion, and healing to those around you. Together, we become agents of positive change, spreading love, fostering mental wellness, and creating a more harmonious world.

As we move forward into the unknown, let us do so with open hearts and a renewed sense of purpose. The path may be winding, but it is illuminated by the radiant glow of love and the promise of shared well-being. With hope as our guiding star, we journey into the uncharted territory of tomorrow, embracing each moment as an opportunity to heal, empower, and cherish the precious bonds that unite us in the beautiful tapestry of life.

LOVING ME LOVING YOU

In the mirror's gaze, we often stray,
Seeking flaws, on this self-critical day.
Yet beyond the surface, beneath the skin,
Lies a beauty, a grace that's found within.

In ourselves, let's learn to see,
The light that shines eternally.
Embrace our flaws, our scars, our grace,
For within our souls, love finds its place.

And as we look into another's eyes,
See beyond their masks, their sweet disguise.
Acknowledge the beauty that's deep inside,
Where love and kindness do abide.

In this journey, let's both find,
The beauty of heart and soul combined.
For it's in loving ourselves, we truly see,
The radiant beauty of you and me.

Books for Couples:

1. "The Seven Principles for Making Marriage Work" by John M. Gottman, PhD and Nan Silver

2. "Hold Me Tight: Seven Conversations for a Lifetime of Love" by Dr. Sue Johnson

3. "The Relationship Cure: A 5 Step Guide to Strengthening Your Marriage, Family, and Friendships" by John M. Gottman, PhD

4. "The 5 Love Languages: The Secret to Love that Lasts" by Gary Chapman

5. "Nonviolent Communication: A Language of Life" by Marshall B. Rosenberg, PhD

6. "Attached: The New Science of Adult Attachment and How It Can Help You Find – and Keep – Love" by Amir Levine and Rachel Heller

7. "The Art of Happiness" by Dalai Lama and Howard Cutler

8. "Getting the Love You Want: A Guide for Couples" by Harville Hendrix, PhD

Online Resources for Couples:

1. The Gottman Institute (https://www.gottman.com/): Offers articles, videos, and workshops on improving relationships based on research by Dr. John Gottman.

2. Emotionally Focused Therapy (EFT) (https://www.iceeft.com/): Provides information and resources on EFT, a therapy approach focused on strengthening emotional bonds in relationships.

3. Psychology Today: Relationships (https://www.psychologytoday.com/us/basics/relationships): Features articles, advice, and therapist directories for couples seeking guidance.

4. BetterHelp (https://www.betterhelp.com/): Offers online therapy and counseling services for individuals and couples dealing with various relationship and mental health challenges.

5. OurRelationship (https://www.ourrelationship.com/): Provides an online program based on research for couples looking to improve their relationships.

6. The Five Love Languages Quiz (https://www.5lovelanguages.com/): Helps individuals and couples understand their love languages and improve communication.

International Resources for Couples:

1. Relate (UK) (https://www.relate.org.uk/): Offers relationship support and counselling services in the United Kingdom.

2. Relationships Australia (https://www.relationships.org.au/): Provides relationship support, counselling, and education in Australia.

3. eNotalone (Canada) (https://www.enotalone.com/): An online community and resource centre for relationship advice, particularly in Canada.

4. Retrouvaille International (https://www.retrouvaille.org/): Offers a program designed to help couples rediscover their relationship's joy, particularly in the United States.

5. Marriage Care (Ireland) (https://www.marriagecare.ie/): Provides marriage preparation and relationship counseling services in Ireland.

6. Couples Counselling Singapore (https://couplescounseling.com.sg/): Offers relationship counseling services in Singapore.

These resources encompass a wide range of approaches to support couples in their journey toward healing, growth, and improved mental well-being.